RESTAURANT...

FOR REAL

Published by Mindstir Media, LLC
45 Lafayette Rd | Suite 181| North Hampton, NH 03862 | USA
1.800.767.0531 | www.mindstirmedia.com

Printed in the United States of America
ISBN-13: 978-1-7332346-9-6
Library of Congress Control Number: 2019908907

RESTAURANT...
FOR REAL

MICHELLE ESTES

MINDSTIR MEDIA

DEDICATION

This book is dedicated to a Restaurant and a Recipe

Thank you to my staff...The Ingredients
Without you, these stories would not be so flavorful

Thank you to my regulars...The Mixers
If you're wondering, yes, I am writing about you

Thank you to my family...The Tasters
They endured countless hours of me telling these stories

I've written this recipe
Good luck with the measurements

When life gives you lemons...
Make lemonade.

MY MOTHER HAD THAT BOOK, it was always in my room. It was written by Erma Bombeck. I honestly never read it but apparently the title alone was enough to hone my problem solving skills. Sweeten the sour.

Being a chef I believe is 50% talent. Yes, you have to have the basic skills to put together flavors and profiles of food. If you have the knack, you will always grow and learn. The other 50% is being able to execute, problem solve and think on your feet. You have to be able to change courses at the last minute and still reach your shore. Accept a challenge and conquer it. There are no problems... only solutions. Always adapt. Lead your people with confidence and they will follow with perfection. There is never the word "can't" only "what can?"

Climb high, high as you can, when you fall, climb again. You know what to avoid this time. Eventually you will get there. Believe most importantly in everything and that all is possible. Only then can you be truly GREAT!

CONTENTS

PREFACE

HALLOWEEN 2001... OPENING NIGHT. It is the perfect time of year to open. The cool autumn breeze swept away the usual sweltering humidity in the air. Everything was in check for our gala grand opening. We were Mobile's newest casual fine-dining restaurant, in the heart of downtown. We opened with a staff of select seasoned professionals, each bringing years of experience in their specialty in this field. Spirits were soaring.

The kitchen is in high gear, preparing a spread of hors d'oeuvres, sampling the flavors of our exquisite menu offerings. The front of the house is bustling around polishing and preparing everything to the finest detail, ensuring the guests will be amazed by the five-star experience that is to come. The bar is... nothing... doing nothing.

Yes, we have specialty cocktails to prepare, yes the wine list is incredible, or at least it's going to be. But it's four o'clock and we are still waiting on a liquor license. Although we had been approved, we had yet to get our physical license at the restaurant. Until that piece of paper is in hand, we can in no shape, form, or fashion open this bar.

Tension is mounting. How can we open without serving any booze? Mobile is a drinking town. Happy hour is almost a religion. We might as well tell people not to breathe. The owner is in Montgomery, our state capital, at the ABC (Alabama Beverage Control) office trying to fix whatever had happened. I am at the restaurant, waiting for his call.

The guests are beginning to arrive. The list was comprised of the people in this town who can make or break any new restaurant. Servers pass hors d'oeuvres, soft big band music plays, the atmosphere is impressive. Still no booze. I am beginning to sweat, and not due to the weather. I mingle with the guests, trying to converse on anything to divert their attention from the fact they don't have a cocktail in their hand.

As the late great Bette Davis would say "Fasten your seatbelts...

It's going to be a bumpy night." We are not going to get any kind of rave reviews without booze. It's the kiss of death. Waiting, waiting, sweating, waiting... RING. It's him... Finally, the liquor license is in his hand. The bar is open! Let the festivities begin.

Welcome, we are embarking on a journey through the restaurant world. ...FOR REAL. A world where nothing is as easy as it seems. Where behind the scenes, more mayhem is going on than you could ever imagine while on the surface it is somehow flawless. Climb aboard. You're about to take a ride through those back-room doors and meet some interesting characters along the way. Fasten your seatbelts. It's going to be bumpy.

CH. 1
THE INGREDIENTS

THE OPENING BEHIND US, we quickly became established as a go-to place downtown. Everyone loved the atmosphere. We were the first place to have a huge courtyard. Dining alfresco was gaining popularity in Mobile. Our bar was designed to make patrons feel like they were in the courtyard, only with much-needed air conditioning. We had primo drink specials and started the three-martini lunch trend. The food was amazing. During happy hour you could get bar bites and small tapas-style snacks, another trend we started. And the staff... they made everyone feel at home, and everyone loved them. You couldn't have asked for better. We had all the ingredients for success.

Now, most people would consider my staff the biggest shit-show on earth if they really knew what was going on behind those doors, and I certainly am not eliminating myself by any means. To us, it was business as usual. There is no room for normalcy in this business. If you're looking for that, I'm sure there is a cubicle at some accounting firm with your name on it. We were family, a little dysfunctional, but still family. A family we chose, a family we proudly belonged to and a family that stuck together no matter what the circumstances. Who else was going to put up with us?

Through the years, we had our ups and downs. We had our good times and bad. We had scary moments, hysterical moments, sad moments, and flat-out crazy times. Each of us joined the family from different circumstances, different stages in our lives and for different reasons. Everyone offered a unique flavor to the mix. We were like the perfect recipe, and the dish wouldn't be complete if one ingredient was missing. Once you became a part of the family, there was a bond in this crew that no one could break.

We had our random people that came and went. They just couldn't hang with the crew. But in spite of all our idiosyncrasies and craziness, we were serious. I feel like the most fortunate person on earth to have been so blessed with such a great group that treated the restaurant like they owned it themselves. I never considered them employees, they were friends. I was their co-worker, not their boss.

We always said that we should save our videos. We had a sitcom going on behind those doors, never a dull moment. We wouldn't know what to do with that. So here are the stories, true accounts, real people, and situations. Truth is better than fiction, and FOR REAL... you can't make this shit up.

Chelle

I'll start this list of ingredients with myself. I haven't always been a restaurant person. I started my career path in life in the retail world. All I wanted to do was go to fashion school. I wanted to be a great American fashion designer. Well, my father had different plans. I was going to go to college and get a "real" degree. Now he considered a real degree something like engineering, med school, law school, etc., but he settled for a business degree. This "fashion thing" as he called it was not happening. So, I went to our local college and got a BS in marketing.

After graduation, my parents sent me to Paris to study fashion finally. When I returned home, I packed my bags and moved to San Francisco to follow my dreams. After a few years out there, I came home to Mobile. My mother had fallen ill, and I wanted to spend what time she had left with her. She helped me open my own little clothing boutique in the up and coming downtown area, and I started designing dresses. It was awesome, but it didn't pay the bills. So I did what every other starving artist does, and got a job waiting tables.

My first job was at a late-night dive called Eggheads that catered to all the drunks when the bars closed down. I'd never had any experience in hospitality, but I thought, how hard can it be? Just get them some food, sober them up. Turns out I sucked at it. After one shift they moved me to their bar down the street to try my hand at making drinks instead. I was much better at that and learned the art of high-volume service. A few weeks later, one of the owners came into the bar and profusely apologized to me for having to fire me. What? Let me get this straight—I got fired? From Eggheads? Okay, I guess I really did suck at waiting tables that bad. So, bartending was my thing, and so were numbers and organization. I quickly became the girl that the bar and restaurant owners hired to set up their businesses. I did inventory control, food and liquor costs, payroll and just about everything else you could imagine. From sports bars to strip clubs, I did it all. Guess that college education paid off. Thanks, Dad.

Time passed, and the fashion world still wasn't paying the bills. Then one day I got a call from a friend of mine. He was opening a new restaurant downtown. Casual in the dress code and atmosphere, but fine dining in terms of food, white tablecloths, and service. He needed a manager. I accepted the job. Little did I know how much that call would change my life.

Byron

Byron and I first met when I had my little retail store downtown. I was designing cute little hippie-style dresses. I could sew, but couldn't draw, and he was an awesome artist. He would draw my dresses for me. When the restaurant opened, we were the original managers there. We worked side by side. We were the best of friends.

When the day came that the restaurant was up for sale, we bought it together. It was the obvious choice, as we had been running it since it opened. Both of us were front of the house. We quickly realized that one of us needed to be back of the house. At first, it was primarily Byron. I only did a couple of shifts. He could cook, but home cooking and restaurant service lines are two totally different animals. After one busy Valentine's night, his kitchen days were over. He just did not have the organizational skills it took to run a line. I moved to the back of the house full-time, leaving Byron to run the front.

He had the people to help him. Ella, was his manager. She was awesome. Got shit done. Then he decided he wanted to be totally in charge and fired her. The first of many poor decisions he made. He wasn't a leader, especially not a leader by example. He could never get a bank ready for the bartender by eleven o'clock when we opened. They would have to bring their own money to make change for the customers until he got there, usually after lunch. Byron couldn't get the next week's schedule out before half the week was over. Thank God our staff would just show up Tuesday through Thursday— well most of the time. He was just as unorganized in the front of the house. He needed a manager and fired the best right hand he could have had.

He really didn't want to work, and when he was the manager on duty, he was never available. It's hard to manage your own restaurant from a barstool at the bar next door. Because of all this, the servers had little to no respect for him.

He was raised with a silver spoon. Given everything all his life, including his parents' money for his part of the restaurant. That was more than my investment, giving him a 1% advantage of ownership. His boyfriend enabled this lackadaisical personality as well. Byron never had to pay a bill in his life. Couldn't even tell you an average power bill cost. He didn't have a checking account until he was forty-five! Spoiled! It shouldn't have shocked me that his work ethic was less than subpar.

Our relationship deteriorated over the years. Even though he was gay, I felt like I was in a marriage. A marriage that started as best friends then turned south and kept going downhill. It was sad.

Ella

It was happy hour at the bar. This was the time between manager and owner of the restaurant. I wasn't currently working there. Byron and I had come in to have a glass of wine and in walked this cute girl, dressed in a professional dress and heels. She went to the bar and told the bartender that she had a job interview with the owner. Well, there's not a snowball's chance in hell. At the time he was ready to sell and had pretty much checked out. He usually let his voice mail stay full so he would not be bothered with any messages. There she sat, all prim and proper, legs crossed, shoulders back, sipping some water... waiting. We were the only people in the bar and started talking with her. I wanted to know her story. Turns out she had just moved back to Mobile, and not by choice. She was a Katrina refugee. She had been managing a restaurant in New Orleans when the hurricane hit and had evacuated to Mobile. Like most refugees, she had no restaurant, no home, nothing to go home to. New Orleans wasn't going to be back for quite some time. She knew that she would be in Mobile for a while.

There she sat, still waiting. It had been about an hour now. We sat there chit-chatting. I had pretty much already interviewed her. She was perfect—fine dining experience, plus diners, dives, and bars. She was originally from Mobile with big family and Mardi Gras ties. The girl was gold. I had offered to buy her a glass of wine earlier which she politely declined. After about two hours, still sipping water and waiting, it was obvious he wasn't coming. She finally accepted a glass of wine, and we chatted some more. I just loved her, good vibes. She finished her wine, gave the bartender her contact information and left. I immediately called the owner and told him he needed to hire this girl. He did, and she was awesome. My first hire and I didn't even own the place yet. At least I knew when I bought it, it came with a great manager!

I could tell so many stories on a personal note about Ella. She became one of my closest friends. We had our own language, could finish each other's sentences, and have a whole conversation without muttering more than two words. But this story is about the restaurant so I will focus on that. At work, she was all business. Everyone loved her. She managed the staff. We planned the banquets together. She worked her ass off, and was very serious.

After Byron stupidly fired her, she went back to New Orleans to try to rebuild her life there. She came back a year later because it just wasn't the same. New Orleans still had a way to go in the rebuilding process. She took a job managing a corporate retail store, but the restaurant business gets in your soul. What's that song? You can check out any time you like, but you can never leave. Without even consulting Byron, I hired her to work Saturday brunches in the kitchen with us. It broke up the monotony of the day-to-day corporate grind.

She had now become a kitchen bitch, and she rocked it! She was in charge of pizzas, salads, French toast and usually the specials. And yes, she took that one-day-a-week job very seriously too. She was good, especially to have never worked in the back of the house before. It was her idea to freeze the orange and cranberry juice in the ice trays, so it didn't dilute the champagne for us. We took champagne thirty (that magic time thirty minutes before your shift was up and you started to clean and wrap it up) very seriously!

She joined a Mardi Gras organization when she returned and became highly involved with them. That was a huge plus as these groups, especially the women's groups, would come in with parties of twenty-five to forty people to do brunches. They could become a little crazy once they took to the champagne, sometimes getting a little impatient about their food. Ella would often step in and be "me," and calm them right down. After all, she was one of them. She was our little refugee. At least something good came out of that hurricane.

Kameron

Kameron was our banquet manager. I flat-out stole him from this diner down the street. Ella and I went in to eat one day, and he was our server. We clicked right away. We told him to meet us at this little bar around the corner after his shift, and we'd buy him a drink. Next thing we knew he was part of our family. I didn't really know what to do with him when he first started, but he was organized and awesome with people. I decided to make him our banquet manager. He could deal with all those parties and weddings in his sleep. And the fact he was gay didn't hurt one bit. Those women loved him. I loved the fact that he had catering experience. That was an area that I wanted to grow, and he grew it. I loved doing off-premise events with him. It was always a new adventure. When I started to stress, he'd calm me right down.

He was always jumping in to help with whatever needed to be done. He was awesome in the kitchen, and we could always count on him when we were short. He was the original "Chicken Bitch," making the chicken and waffles across the kitchen. He streamlined this process before Fynn came on board.

Kameron was my right hand. We quickly became the best of friends.

We seemed to have our own language, could have a whole conversation without saying a word. It was the closest to Ella I've ever encountered. We would take our vacations together. Our place was Panama. We spent many weeks there. We both dreamed of eventually retiring there. If it weren't for Kameron, the front of the house would have been a mess. He always held it together.

Kameron never had a car, and didn't care. He was a downtown guy. He lived with Toni around the corner from the restaurant. He could be there at the drop of a hat. He spent as much time at the restaurant as me. I'd stay with them on really busy weekends, especially during Mardi Gras. Those nights usually entailed some drinking. We'd sneak into the house trying to be quiet, so we didn't wake Toni up. That never really worked, and we'd end up in trouble. Everybody loved Kameron. He never really stressed out, always even-keeled.

Duane

Duane was one of those people that we watched grow. He started with us as a dishwasher. It wasn't long before he was on the kitchen crew. He had two stints. The first being very short-lived. Seriously, how many times can your grandmother die in two months? I'm guessing it's not four. By the time we hired him for the second go around, he had grown. He was married, had a beautiful son, and really had learned the sense of responsibility. He came back as kitchen crew and quickly became my right hand. He was the person I could depend on. I felt confident leaving him in charge, knowing he would lead the crew and get the shit done. He was over six feet tall and had the build of a professional basketball player. That was the best thing because he could reach everything in the kitchen. The girls called him "the ladder."

How lucky was I to have this awesome, dependable person? Well... luck eventually runs out. His wife had been having an affair, and he was distraught, trying to keep his family together. He was in New Orleans at a food show one weekend when they wandered into one of the local strip clubs. There on the pole was this stripper that was about to throw a big, fat curveball into his life. She was a scrawny little thing and all eighty pounds of her tempted him. He was already upset with his marriage situation and enjoyed the attention. He may have even thought about cheating himself, but never got the chance. After a few drinks with some thigh rubbing and a sob story, she convinced him to let her ride back to Mobile with him so she could visit her mom, who of course was "sick."

Little did he know, she had a whole other agenda. She just wanted a ride to transport cocaine back to Mobile and make an easy five grand. She figured if the situation went awry, it was his car, she'd be fine. Well, Duane met her the next morning, and off they went. He had a tail light out and got pulled over about twenty minutes outside Mobile. Next thing you know the cops are searching their bags, which Duane had no problem with until they found the three kilos of cocaine that she had slipped into his bag. Of course, she was "shocked!"

So, Duane was in jail and facing drug trafficking charges. He was family, and it was time for the family to pull together. He had always been there for me, and I was damn sure going to be there for him. We hired the best criminal defense attorney in this town, and the Free-Duane project commenced. It took a while to get a court date set. While he sat in jail, we all wrote to him to inspire him. (In the meantime, his wife ran off with her boyfriend and divorced him.)

I had prepaid postcards printed with the return address, "what doesn't kill you makes you stronger" on them. They sat at the register, and everyone would write to him whenever they felt like it. We kept him abreast of all the goings on and most importantly how much we loved him and were awaiting his return. Even the regular customers would write him. I must have mailed thirty postcards a week. I even figured out how to print pictures on them. He was definitely the most popular convict at mail call. We started a commissary fund for him, and everybody would throw money in the jar, again, including the regulars. I would deposit this money in his jail account once a week. It seemed like forever, but finally, the court date came.

We flooded the courthouse. The entire staff of the restaurant, his family, his really great friends, most of which were dedicated military. It was standing room only. I had already, at the request of his attorney, written to the judge to plead his case and described what a responsible, upstanding man he was. I was one of his character witnesses, and when I got up to talk to the judge, I begged her to understand that he was a victim of bad decisions, and not some two-bit drug addict. In the end, she saw that he had a world of positive people in his life and that maybe he would learn from this and become a better person. She released him from jail, on a strict work release program. He had to wear an ankle bracelet and was only allowed to go from home to work. I became best friends with his probation officer, as I had to submit his schedule to him weekly and call him if there were any changes. Six months he wore that fine jewelry and then it was over. Though still on probation, he was free of the shackle.

Duane had made one stupid decision, but we had him back. (By the way, the stripper got a slap on the wrist and was set free). He grew even more that year and only became a better man. If I had ever had a child of my own, I would have been proud to have Duane.

Erica

The best kitchen bitch ever! Erica was from a little resort town in New England called Falmouth, just outside of Boston. She was dating a guy in the Coast Guard who had gotten transferred down here in Mobile. She came to visit him and had decided to move down here with him if she could find a job. So, she came in to apply with us. She got there around two thirty, the ideal, appropriate time for a restaurant, in between lunch and dinner service. Any seasoned restaurant person knows this. We, at the time, did not need any kitchen help. We actually had a good set crew. I was in the office, doing paperwork and was told that someone was here to apply for a kitchen job. Okay, give him an application, I'll look over it later. I was informed that it wasn't a he, but a she. That was a game changer, tell her to wait. I'll be right out to talk to her. Never pass up the opportunity to talk to a kitchen bitch. Girls rock it.

I immediately loved her. She had tons of experience, personality, was as cute as ever and could offer that New England flair to our team. I had to hire her. I'd figure out how to work her in. You just don't let talent like that walk out the door. I took her application and told her I'd be in touch with her soon. I immediately went to call her previous boss for a reference, short of her being wanted for murder, she was hired. My first call… "Ohhhh, you got my girl." 'Nuf said. I called her and told her to show up the next day. She hadn't even pulled out of the parking lot yet… Soon enough? When I went on shift later that night in the kitchen, the guys asked me if I had shown her the kitchen. Are you kidding? I wanted her to start working here, not scare her away! We had the smallest kitchen in the world. I figured I had a better chance of her staying if I got her here, in kitchen clothes, ready to work. (That worked, by the way)

At the time, I was still going back and forth, front and back of the house. So was Byron. The next day was Valentine's Day, one of the single busiest nights in the restaurant industry. It was my turn to hostess and Byron's turn to expedite in the kitchen. We were booked solid! There was no room for walk-ins. Most tables were flipping two or three times. BUSY! Erica came in, saw the kitchen, and stayed! Yay! We didn't expect too much from her that night but figured she could do some prep and be the extra hand. She would at least see how this tiny kitchen operates on such a busy night.

Everything was running smoothly on my end, seating the reservations on time to flow the kitchen right. Not so much on Byron's end. He was expediting and had become very flustered when all these tickets started coming in. They were two tops, for God's sake. Easy! But too much for him, so next thing you know I'm back there in a formal gown and heels (not the first time, wouldn't be the last) trying to run the line. I needed to get back to the hostess stand. He was not dressed for that job. I asked Erica if she could jump in and she said sure. She'd never worked this line or seen ANY of the food plated. Shit, she'd only been there about three hours. It's the busiest night of the year… Why not? Sure! She jumped right in the deep end and treaded water like a pro! Never even went under. She ran that line all night and never missed a beat. She was gold! Even better, she showed up to work the next day!

I put her on the schedule on as many kitchen shifts as I could and filled in her hours with two nights in the front of the house waiting tables. She had never waited tables before and took to that like a pro as well. In the kitchen, she was the bomb. She ran it like a well-oiled machine. She could rock any station. She didn't take any bullshit either. Don't do some half-ass job for her. She'd been known to throw an entire plate of food on the floor and make you start over. A perfectionist and you'd better measure up.

She was a Red Sox fan, and had a huge tattoo of the socks on her shoulder. She never missed a game. She rigged up her computer in the kitchen and no one disturbed her with idle chit-chat during the games. On the floor, she was so charming. What? Erica?... To the customers—at least to their faces. One woman even called her delightful. Okay, I can think of many words to describe Erica, but delightful? Boy, did she have these people snowed. She even had a pleasant, sweet phone voice, like this whole other person. When the day came that she could have moved to full-time in the kitchen, she declined. She had become used to the change of pace, not to mention the money, of waiting tables. She did cook-offs with us, promotions and especially beer tastings (because I know squat about beer). She was a team player and a huge part of the crew.

Then sadly, the time came that her fiancé (yes, they had gotten engaged) was transferred back to New England. We were sad to see her go. She was irreplaceable. But we now had a reason to take a restaurant road trip up for the wedding. Which we did! She was our girl for a long while. Then New England got her back. Almost unscathed, except for the "y'all" that had embedded into her vocabulary. She'd always deny it, but it slipped out like butter. Erica, our little Yankee Red Sox girl!

Katie

Our happy hour crowd was a tough sell. The right bartender was key. One of their favorites (and mine) was Katie. We hired her in a moment of desperation when she came in to apply on a day our bartender was a no-show. It was simply a case of right place, right time. Her interview consisted of, "Make a cosmo," which she fumbled around behind the bar finding the ingredients and did it to perfection. Hired!

She would have all the customers drinks ready and sitting at their spot when they walked in the door. She knew all their quirks, and there were so many of them. A specific glass, lime with no rind, half a pack of Sweet'N Low, two ice cubes, half salted rim... the list goes on and on. On the rare occasion she would take off work, she actually had a list for her fill-in. It was like a seating chart, with who sat in which chair and their specific drink.

Everybody loved her. She was a true team player. She worked in the kitchen with us on brunches and organized rotating the staff for that shift. She became Kameron's right hand, okay his bitch: planning and setting up banquets, helping with the schedule, organizing special events, etc. She was good at anything she did.

She started working at the restaurant when Duane was in jail, and although she had never met him, she would throw money from her tips into his fund jar. She figured if everybody else loved and supported him so much, he must be an awesome guy. Turns out, when Duane got out of jail and came back to us, there was an instant connection between them. She was a huge basketball fan, very athletic. They just looked good together. Not too much of a football fan, which was to my advantage. I could always count on her to be the one person that would sport a 49ers jersey with me. Usually, you frown on employees dating each other, but they were my power couple. They may have had arguments (what couple doesn't), but you'd never know it. They were always on point at work.

When Kameron and I would leave for our Panama adventures, she and Duane were in charge. I used to make her sign a statement saying that she wouldn't quit while we were gone when Byron started driving her crazy, which he would every time. I trusted her and Duane with everything and felt confident when things were in their hands.

Toni

Toni was one of the most colorful servers who ever worked there. Literally. She had massive tattoos and different color streaks in her hair that regularly changed. She was ex-military and definitely had her own way of doing things. I had actually tried to hire (okay, steal) her many times before she finally joined our crew. She bartended at one of the oldest established bars downtown. She set up a Bloody Mary bar with all the fixin's every Sunday there. I actually stole the idea of our Bloody Mary bar from her.

After some scene where she allegedly had a guy in a choke hold with a pool cue (something her employer frowned on and didn't think was so cute), she came to us. She could wait on the entire bar and courtyard by herself. She was a little brash, would have never won Miss Congeniality, but she was awesome. She was the only person there who could call me out and tell me when I was being a bitch. I admit I was a little scared of her. I'm glad she loved me. You didn't ever want to be on her bad side. She had her regular customers and brought most of them with her.

She bonded the crew, always planning events and "family" outings. We'd usually rent a bus, and the crew would go on all sorts of adventures, from tubing down the river to bowling. Her favorite thing was theme days on Sundays. I loved her for that. Any excuse for me to wear a tutu to work. We would dress up and go all out. One of my favorite themes was superhero day. It was one of our friend's son's tenth birthday, and he wanted to be Captain America. She planned this whole party for him at the restaurant, and we all dressed up as our favorite superheroes. She even got some of the regular customers involved. He had a great party that day. She was so creative.

Kameron and Toni were roommates. They lived right around the corner from the restaurant, which was a convenient thing (well for me). They were both members of the DSDs (Dauphin Street Drunks) a pirate-themed Mardi Gras foot-marching society. She was all about that. Any excuse for her to wear a corset. Their house might as well have been floating in the bay. It was decked out pirate all the way.

Fynn

Fynn was the best guy I've ever picked up at a bar. I was at one of our local favorite watering holes. It was your typical neighborhood pub where you know everyone. For some reason, I was talking to a friend of mine about sewing something. Out of nowhere, this guy makes a comment that if you cut the fabric on the bias, it will flow better. Now I'd never seen this guy before, and I was intrigued. He was sitting down the bar by himself having a beer. He was young (20s), cute and knew about sewing? I had to get up and go sit next to him. I mean who is he and what's his story? Obviously he was gay.

I sat next to him, and we started chit-chatting. He was working at a gas station at the time, not really loving it. I had a good vibe from him. At the time we were in desperate need of someone to work in the kitchen for Sunday brunch. He said he would be interested although he didn't have any relevant kitchen experience. After a few drinks, I figured what the hell. If he was serious I told him to show up Sunday morning ready to work. I really had nothing to lose in this situation. I thought he was gay, so if he did show up, and didn't work out in the kitchen, I potentially found Kameron a cute new boyfriend.

He actually showed up. He was wearing holey jeans, a wife beater (a thin-ribbed usually very fitted tank top meant to be worn under a shirt, not as a shirt) and a doo-rag (what we Southerners refer to as a bandana). It was an interesting ensemble, to say the least. The rest of the kitchen staff was giving me shit. Really? You just hired this guy you picked up in a bar? As if they didn't pick up the last three girls they slept with in a bar. At least this was professional-ish.

I admit, he was a little eccentric and the guys didn't take to him at first, but he jumped right in and did a really great job. In spite of the not-so-warm welcome (except from Kameron and me. Yes, Kameron thought he was cute too), he kept showing up every Sunday. Fynn was our official "Chicken Bitch." Kameron even brought him new doo-rags with little chickens and roosters on them, which he wore with pride. We had created a whole new chicken and waffle station on the other side of the kitchen with a baby fryer and waffle iron. He took pride in creating the perfectly seasoned batter for the chicken. I really liked him. He was good people. Eventually, the kitchen crew came around and he became one of us. Poor guy. Eventually, we added Saturday to his schedule, as our brunch got busier. Before you knew it, he quit his gas station job. He was full-time, part of the crew.

By the way, he and Kameron never hooked up. Turned out he wasn't gay. Even has a child now with his long-term girlfriend. Yes, that chicken-doo-rag-wearing, wife-beater-sporting motherfucker. Who says you can't pick up a good man at a bar?

Cody

Well, Cody worked there by default. He was Byron's nephew and started washing dishes for us when he was fifteen. He really didn't have much of a choice, he was family. He was a little cocky at first, just a smart-ass kid. We moved him to the kitchen after we hired Paco, one of his best friends. That's when he started to grow and learn a real sense of responsibility. The challenges of the kitchen became like a game to him. He was always the first one to want to know ticket times as if he was beating his own personal score. He learned everything. You could put him at any station, and he would rock it to perfection.

He was also our comic relief. He could take the most stressful situation and have you dying laughing by the end. He was obsessed with Magic Mike and would run around humping every pole in the kitchen. He was a walking comedy-show hormone.

He brought us all the boys. They were a tight-knit group of friends. They all went to school together, played football, good kids. For most of them, it was their first job. Cody and Paco were kitchen crew, and the rest of the boys would rotate as back servers on Saturdays and Sundays. Cody was the leader of the pack. As he got older, he grew into a well-rounded, caring, responsible man. No longer was he the little adolescent shit we first hired. He was part of the kitchen crew and was definitely a team player.

Paco

The youngest of our kitchen crew was Paco. He was one of Cody's best friends. He was our Mexican boy. He started working with us when he was sixteen, his first job. Originally, he was our dishwasher but quickly moved into the kitchen. Paco and I were the two who ran the line on our Sunday brunches. We were a team, crammed together with really no room to breathe. We had a rhythm. The kitchen dance. He was the one the servers could always talk to and find out the status of whatever order they were questioning.

Paco was laid back. He would get shit done but would take his time. He never could be at work on time, not in the mornings anyway. We used to count down the minutes on Sunday mornings. The deal was, if you were late, you had to clean the kitchen by yourself. The magic time was thirty minutes. So as the clock ticked away, and when time had past, sure enough, Paco would waltz in, usually in his Alabama pajama pants, as he had just rolled out of bed. He knew, kitchen-cleaning duty solo. Sunday was a bitch too. The kitchen looked like a tornado had spun through it. Cases of eggshells piled in the corner, and shit everywhere. We'd all be spent and go outside to take a much-needed break, and Paco would go back in and get it started. He always had a good attitude about it.

He was a strong team player and very serious about how plates should look and be presented. He was great on the line, the servers could actually talk to him, he never got hot-headed. He was always calm and always smiling. Our little Mexican.

Monty

I flat-out stole Monty from the restaurant next door. He started just on Sundays and very quickly moved into full-time with us. He was an interesting character, to say the least. On the surface, to look at him, he was a little scary. He had crazy, long, curly hair, the huge gauge earrings, and was covered in tattoos. He rode a skateboard to work. He would get in and immediately put on the most godawful music. You would think he lived in the hood. I spent most of my time on shift with him tuning him out. He knew it and would strike up conversations just to try to get a rise out of me.

He was crazy, but he was good. We were the first kitchen that allowed him some creativity. I put him in charge of our prime rib. He was our grill man, so that was a key brunch item for his station. At first, he was nervous with his prep, wanting to know exactly what to do. He was used to a very regimented kitchen. We had our signature items that had specific recipes, but there were certain things you could just go with. We liked the fact that the prime rib was seasoned a little differently each week. So did the customers, some of whom ate there every week. Once he had the green light to go, he shined. He was so creative, he recreated our breakfast tacos recipe, added some flair to our mashed potatoes, changed up our au jus.

He was on it.

He loved it when I put him in charge of the soup of the day. He could literally create anything he wanted and took that task very seriously. I don't know why no other kitchen gave him that freedom because he was amazing. They may have been intimidated by his look, but that just goes to show, you can't judge a book by its cover. Monty, our renegade guy.

Amber

Amber was our main bartender. She came to us after a messy divorce and needed a job. She had the personality and looks, so we hired her. She was a spitfire. Everybody loved her. She instigated the entire staff to call me Momma. Every year she would get the staff together and make me a Mother's Day card. It was like having twenty children. She had a little girl who was the most precious thing since sliced bread.

Amber could never decide which team she was batting for. She went through strings of girlfriends, most of them psycho, and then back with her ex-husband. On the surface, she seemed to have it all and the bag of chips, but she was like the little girl with the little curl. When she was good, she was very, very good and when she was bad...

She was our only bartender to go to jail over carding an underage kid working undercover for the ABC (Alabama Beverage Control). Yes, carding him. His birthday showed he was one day away from turning twenty-one. Literally, by midnight she would have been fine, but she got confused on the date and the next thing you know they were dragging her to jail in the middle of her shift. I'll elaborate on the ABC Board later, but suffice it to say, they are dicks. Give a person a badge, and it suddenly makes up for their lack of penis size.

She had a big heart, always putting everyone else first. She was in New York one New Year's Eve and did the wish confetti for everyone in our restaurant family. Amber was the sweetest person you'd ever want to know.

Lukas

Lukas was a professional waiter. He had worked in fine dining all his life. He came to us after working at one of the most elite fine-dining steakhouses in Mobile for twenty-three years. I was shocked when he came in the door to apply, and no I don't need an application. We know who you are. Can you start tomorrow? For whatever reason, he was ready to sever ties with them and move on. Bring it.

He wasn't high volume, mind you. He could only handle a very limited number of tables. And God, don't give him a large party. He could take three two-top tables a night and make more money in tips than servers running around waiting on twenty. He upsold everything. When Lukas was your server, you would have a dining experience. He started you with an appetizer, succulently described it to make you count every second until its arrival at your table. Then, of course, you had to have a salad. Next, he chose a bottle of wine that paired perfectly with your entrée selections. And of course, dessert, with his famous "Lukie" cocktail. He was a pro. Just don't let him pull his own food out of the window. He couldn't see those tickets to save his life.

He was the most requested server we had. He also was the most unrequested. Yes sometimes, people just wanted to come in and grab a bite fast, they would specifically tell us they did not have time to dine with Lukas that night, but they loved him.

He was a generous soul and had at one time shone in the tennis circuit. He taught tennis lessons to children who could not otherwise afford them. He was highly involved with his church. He began a Hot Dogs for Humanity mission. Every Monday, when the restaurant was closed, he set up a booth and gave away hot dogs. Donations were accepted, but not required. This money would go to his church. We always gave him the leftover bottled water from Sunday for his booth. Our regular customers started to give him donations at the restaurant. He was able to begin to offer cheese and chili with his hot dogs. He was so excited. Then one of them had huggers made for him to give out "Hot Dogs for Humanity." The local news featured him as one of Mobile's "Angels." He cried. He was an emotional man. He would give you the shirt off his back if you needed it. We were so fortunate to have him on our team.

Marleena

The only server that was with us from day one to the end was Marleena. She was our friend from San Sebastian, Spain. She really didn't need to work. She just thought it was fun. She worked one day a week, Sunday. I know, rough schedule, right? Her English was pretty good, but it was easy to lose her in translation sometimes. I loved her, but she drove me crazy.

She was a fashionista, always dressed in her own unique style, with her hair perfectly tossed in a casual messy way. She didn't walk, she sashayed. Very classy. Now you would think she was some snooty bitch, but you couldn't be further from the truth. She was the sweetest thing and so down to earth. She drove an old Mustang convertible, and her drink of choice was Budweiser. Not too hard to please.

Of all the years she was with us, she never could do her checkout. We finally gave up, and someone just did it for her. She, like Lukas, couldn't handle too many tables, yet she worked in the bar every Sunday, the busiest section in the restaurant. Thank God she worked with Toni. Toni ran around waiting on most of the tables and Marleena sashayed around waiting on her people. Yes, she had a regular clientele that would only allow her to wait on them. They loved her. It didn't matter that she really didn't know the menu or what a sauce choron was, she could sell it anyway. She was classy. A nice change of pace to our little restaurant family.

Leah

Leah was my best friend and didn't technically work there, but she was as much part of the crew as anyone on payroll. God love her. She would come in for brunch just to get some food and champagne. Next thing you know she was working. Hostessing, bussing, bartending, waiting tables and even cooking. Now keep in mind, she was my friend who had a "real" job, a pretty serious one, too. She worked with autistic children. She was a saint (by day).

She loved to do fundraisers and was highly involved in benefits and causes. She organized one of the first big events we did in our new banquet room. She set the room up as a hair salon with four or five hairdressers

RESTAURANT... FOR REAL

cutting hair for donations. Long hair was the big thing at the time, especially in the bar restaurant scene. She managed to get almost everybody on board with this cause and donate their hair, including me, and at the time my hair was down to my ass. She also loved to do chef auctions for various events, which was always a good money raiser. We always did anything we could to help her causes.

Leah was a great event planner, too. She went all out with themes and decorations. She was always a big help with our yearly anniversary parties, as they were on Halloween. My favorite was when she did a custom murder mystery dinner party for the restaurant.

So in she would come... Thank God you're here. Yes, she'd be put to work again! What a trooper. She would jump right in. She "worked" at least two brunch shifts a week. She was bartending the day one of my favorite actors came in for brunch, and I almost died! She didn't even know who he was! And she forgot his biscuit! She was so fired... Oh wait, she doesn't work here.

She didn't seem to care that she may or may not be put to work every time she came in. Except for the occasional walk of shame days, you know when it's Sunday morning, and you're still Saturday night. I could never do what she did for a living, but she damn sure could do most everything we did. Love her!

Samantha (Sam)

One of our "one-dayers" on the Saturday brunch crew was another good friend of mine, Sam. She was our local silversmith and had just opened her own art gallery a few blocks from the restaurant. She also took her job very seriously. She was in charge of the grill, temping all the steaks and burgers like a pro. I was amazed at how long she stayed with us, especially since she still worked two nights a week at our local watering hole (where I met Fynn). One of those shifts was Saturday, which threw her into a split double at two different places, working about fifteen hours that day. But she never missed a beat.

Occasionally she would have to expedite when I would move to sauté.

32

If this happened, that meant that someone not usually on the Saturday crew would come in to work the grill. God help that person. It could be intimidating for one of the guys to fill in on Saturdays. Don't give her a medium-well burger before a mid-rare when you had an all-day count, and the mid-rare came in three minutes before. That's the moment when she could make Erica seem like a sweet princess.

Sam was very handy, a regular little MacGyver. Her dad owned a refrigeration service company, and she had grown up around it. She could tinker with just about anything and at least get us through until someone could be called for service. Being creative, she made our courtyard logo tables for us, and they were beautiful. She was awesome to have on Saturdays to prep for banquets that night. Her platter presentations were always off the chain. She was a talker, too. Always had a story. Our artist extraordinaire.

Gina

Gina was a local artist in town. Now she could be a novel on her own, very unique. She was our first "champangel." She actually helped create this title. We hired her to pour champagne, and that was it. We had gotten so busy for brunch that the servers had a hard time keeping up with it and at the time the bottomless champagne was free. So, Gina was going to stand out with floppy hats and crazy outfits. She had her own style. She showed up her first day wearing fairy wings. Yes, she stood out. She flitted around the restaurant in her big, floppy hat, wearing these wings pouring champagne. And the glitter—the girl never left the house without it. If you were drinking champagne, you were leaving the restaurant looking like you'd just pulled an all-nighter at one of the local strip clubs. You were glittified!

Erica and Gina became best friends, and for a hot minute, she got Erica on a glitter kick. We had to stop that quickly. It's one thing to leave the restaurant with glitter on you, a whole different story when it's all over your food.

She was the champagne fairy, and she wore that title well. Then the day came that she decided to spread her wings and go to New Orleans to paint. Before she left us, she made sure we had found the perfect person to replace her, or as close to her as possible. She is, mind you, in a league of her own. She was very serious about the training process. Okay, Gina... Really? Pop and pour! Training done. She turned over her wings, literally, to Ava, the new girl, who immediately proclaimed, "Oh my God, I get to wear angel wings!" From then on we had a new "champangel." Thanks, girls.

Ava

Ava was our second "champangel." She took over when Gina left us. She was beautiful. She looked like a model for Victoria's Secret, especially sporting those angel wings. Smart too. She had a full scholarship in engineering at our local college. Not a whole lot of common sense though. Sometimes the things she said made no sense, but she'd just smile.

One time she came in and had forgotten to wear shoes... Shoes! She had stopped to get gas, gone into some coffee place, and picked up treats at the dog store, barefoot the whole time. When she got to work and put on her wings, she realized—no shoes. We had to scrounge around and find her something.

One day she wanted to branch out and try her hand at Bloody Marys. She made one and asked me to try it. I almost spit it out. It was one of the worst things I had ever tasted. I asked her what she put in it, and she said vanilla vodka. There are many flavored vodkas that you can put into a Bloody, but vanilla? She thought that it would be like tomato soup and sour cream. Okay, Ava, stick to the champagne.

She was the sweetest person you would ever want to meet. She was an attraction at the restaurant. Everyone loved her. The little girls thought she was a fairy princess. Every one of them wanted to get their picture taken with her. The men all had the hots for her, and the women loved her cause she never let their glasses run dry. She and the restaurant were featured in one of our local magazines as an attraction in Mobile not to be missed.

The "champangel" had become an icon in Mobile, and she played the role well. We even had cups printed and t-shirts made. Ava... our little angel.

Valerie (Val)

If you have a great relationship with your suppliers, your life will run so much smoother. I was fortunate enough to have a very good friend of mine, Val, as my wine rep. A wine rep is so important to the workings of the restaurant. They are trained on so many levels and know what pairs with your menu style. It's like having your own personal sommelier on staff.

Val was the best. She knew her product. She created the wine list for us, a list that placed us in Wine Spectator Magazine. (One of two restaurants in Mobile to be listed.) Pretty impressive. She educated our staff and made sure they were comfortably versed in our selections. She knew costs and would make sure we always got the deals. Because our champagne Sunday brunches were so busy, we were the number one account for Cooks in the Southeast. Val locked us into the best deal, got us t-shirts and all kinds of promotional items. She was awesome.

Promotions were her specialty. She planned countless events over the years, many of which I will elaborate on later. She always showed up with all the bells and whistles, oh and the shoes! That girl could be wearing a paper bag, but she'd be sporting her Manolos. On the rare occasion I would get out of kitchen clogs, I'd go shop in her closet. She had more shoes than Imelda Marcos and lucky for me, we wore the same size. We always looked good, and our promotions were always the best.

She pretty much did our wine orders for us. She would get the banquet book and reservation book out each week and figure it out. She knew most of our regular customers and when she saw their names on the reservations, she would make sure we were amply stocked in their wine of choice. We never wanted for anything. Unfortunately (for us) every now and then her company allowed her to take a vacation. I always hated those weeks. She was the number one sales rep, so the only person capable of filling in for her was her boss. That never seemed to work out so much. One time when she was gone, and I actually had to do my own order. It was a nightmare. We had two huge wedding events that weekend, so I called her boss to order my wine. Two pinot grigios, four chardonnays, five cabernets, and three merlots. I assumed he knew these were cases I was ordering. Then I went on with the single bottle order. Well, we all know what the word "assume" means. That's exactly what I got. Maybe I should have specified cases on the banquet wine, but I assumed it was a given. Our order showed up Friday afternoon and guess what I got? Two BOTTLES of pinot grigio, four bottles of chardonnay... you get the gist. That wasn't enough wine to make it through the first hour of the first banquet. It was Friday afternoon, so there was no time to reorder! Somehow, we scrounged up barely enough wine to make it through the weekend. This entailed her boss having to beg, borrow, and steal from about ten other restaurants. Let me clarify—Val handled calling all those accounts. He just ran around and picked them up. Yes, I called her, on her vacation, to fix that. Don't you just love your friends? Val should have been on the payroll. She kept the party going.

The Bitch System

The hierarchy in a restaurant is important to the proper running of things. Every restaurant is different. Ours was a little less formal than the typical corporate structure. We were basically on the bitch system. Starting from the top, I, as the owner, was fortunate enough to have two bitches. Kameron and Duane. Kameron was my right hand, liaison to the front of the house and all the banquets. Duane was my right hand in the kitchen. As far as the kitchens order, Duane had Erica, Erica had Cody, Cody had Paco and Paco had anyone in the dish hole. As for Monty... well he wasn't going to be anyone's bitch. Fynn was the chickens' bitch. The girls, Sam, Ella, and sometimes Leah, were each others' bitches. They only worked on Saturdays anyway.

Front of the house started with Kameron. Katie was his bitch. Katie had Amber, and Toni, like Monty, wasn't going to be anybody's bitch. All the other servers knew she was the head bitch, as far as the waitstaff goes. No one gave her any shit. Byron didn't have a bitch. He was a bitch. Nobody listened to him anyway.

The bitch system worked for us. Everybody knew their place. Once Monty decided that he wanted a bitch, and offered to take Fynn. It just doesn't work like that. Fynn was there first. Time served carried a lot of weight in the system, kinda like prison. Technically, Monty should have been his… okay, tell Monty that. Besides, I technically hired Fynn to be Kameron's bitch, and I'm not talking professionally.

CH. 2
SWEET HOME ALABAMA

MOBILE IS A PORT CITY ON THE GULF COAST. It's over 300 years old, and the birthplace of Mardi Gras. Now, most people think that Mardi Gras began in New Orleans, but any Mobilian will quickly correct you on that fact. Mardi Gras began in Mobile in 1703 as an annual carnival celebration. It is a French Catholic festival. Mardi Gras means Fat Tuesday, the last day of feasting and merriment before the self-sacrifice of Lent, which begins the following day on Ash Wednesday and lasts forty days through Easter. The final countdown starting with the Sunday before Mardi Gras, known as Joe Cain Day, is unique to Mobile. Joe Cain is credited with initiating the procession and parades we celebrate today. The term "Raising Cain" came from this procession, comprised of the "Merry Widows" that go to his grave in our local downtown cemetery each year. Mardi Gras is taken very seriously in Mobile.

Today, the celebration begins in Mobile three weeks before Ash Wednesday. There are parades, Mardi Gras societies, formal balls, a king and queen are chosen. It's a local holiday time, a time of revelry. These societies have been planning all year for these three weeks. Elaborate floats have been designed. The costumes alone are museum pieces created by some of the most influential people in town. Even the schools and banks close for that last week. Feasting and merriment of old have become flat-out debauchery. As all the parades and balls are hosted downtown, any restaurant in that area trying to operate during this time has some unique challenges.

First is the parking. The streets close down, leaving those restaurants trapped in the revelry circle very inaccessible. And yes, we were right in the middle of it. Street vendors and food trucks set up on just about every corner, selling everything you can possibly imagine on a stick. Fair food, and no one is eating any meal on a plate. It's just not Mardi Gras until you've had a corndog. (It's the only time of the year I just have to eat one). We allow open containers on the street, so everyone has cooler in tow with whatever their poison of choice may be. If they were lucky enough to get a parking spot inside the sacred circle, they have a full-service "car bar." Yes, drinking is a huge part of it. It's a three-week drunk fest. Because everyone is about to give up their vices for Lent… Right… Any excuse!

Campers and tailgaters set up shop in every possible parking lot. Makeshift carnival fairs pop up overnight with rides that look like they should have been retired last century. Music blares from every speaker and boombox, kids run around ramped on cotton candy sugar rushes, fighting over parade throws. And the beads! The more, the merrier. It's the one time a year that your status in society is not judged by where you live, your profession, or how much money you make. It's based solely on how many cheap plastic beads are around your neck. And you'd be amazed at what people will flash for those beads. The bigger the balls (on the beads), the more of a titty show you're going to get. Rational people act crazy when those beads start flying off the parade floats.

Then after the parade, the mess. All kinds of shit ends up caught on the street lights, trees, and power lines. Smashed candy and food all are strewn over the ground. Yes, there is an attempt to clean this mess up nightly. But not until Lent has set in, the vendors, food trucks and fairs have moved on and the first hard rain comes to wash away the stench do you really get downtown back to some sort of order… some sort.

Now the bars downtown have it made. Many make over half their profit for the year those three weeks, slinging out overpriced drinks as fast as they can make them. But the restaurants, not so much. One year we took the attitude of if you can't beat 'em… join 'em. We set up a tent in the parking lot and tried to sell fair food. We ordered little baby corndogs and made one of our signature dishes, chicken and waffles, street-style. We got waffle cones and put our chicken strips tossed in honey butter in them. Perfect for walking around. The health department didn't like our little idea so much. They shut that tent down. Oh well, at least we tried something.

The only reason people want to come into a restaurant during Mardi Gras is to use the bathroom. Let's face it, they are much nicer than most of your puke-ridden bars and porta potties. So, we have to establish some sort of order. We put up the traditional "Restrooms are for customers use only" signs. We might as well say, "Blah, blah, blah, blah." We still have to police the doors. The people don't care. We opened for Mardi Gras Day our first year in business. That day culminated with a whopping $129 in sales and an $800 plumbing bill. People will throw anything down a public toilet... how do they live at home? After that we were closed on Mardi Gras Day like every other business in town, except for the downtown bars making their last bucks on that final countdown.

Mardi Gras is unique to this area of the country. It's spread to most cities along the Gulf Coast, New Orleans being next. But it started in Mobile and every year sometime around February we say laissez les bons temps rouler – let the good times roll. And let the restaurants downtown survive it another year.

Hurricanes

Being on the Gulf Coast, every year between June and November, we have to pay attention to the hurricane forecast. Hurricanes seem to get into the warm waters of the Gulf and bounce around like a pinball, finally making landfall anywhere from Florida to Texas. We are right in the middle. You can go years with no major activity, just tropical storms that give everyone an excuse to have a "hurricane party." It means lots of rain, which we're used to anyway. No big deal. When one actually forms and hits anywhere around, we don't take it lightly. It's going to affect business and affect it hard. Once that storm goes into the Gulf, a cone is established by the Weather Bureau. If you're still in that red zone of the cone twenty-four hours before impact and it's a Category 2 or higher, you'd better start implementing your emergency plan.

Our whole front of the restaurant was huge glass windows. We had custom fitted plywood sheets to cover them with and hopefully prevent the glass breakage. The biggest problem for us was the flooding. Mobile is below sea level anyway, and downtown was right on the water. It would flood during a regular old rainstorm. Add the hurricane factor... you're getting some water. And finally, we had to deal with power outages. Again, this could happen anytime, but it's guaranteed to be down at least a week if a hurricane hits within a hundred miles of your location. It's not just the city it makes landfall in, but the feeder bands that whip the winds for miles around that are equally as devastating, sometimes more so. When you have an area with a bunch of closed businesses, you, unfortunately, have looters. You have to check on your investment constantly to hopefully avoid this problem.

We had a two-year stint where two major hurricanes hit around us. Ivan in Pensacola, Florida, and Katrina in Gulfport, Mississippi. Both of these storms caused some major damage in our area as well and caused the downtown businesses to be closed for at least a week each time. Hurricanes are devastating, but it's amazing how it bonds people together. Everyone helps each other out to get back up and running. We all looked out for each other.

The only positive thing about the hurricane aftermath is you eat like a king. Once we lose power, and someone could get into downtown in a truck that wouldn't stall in the flood waters, we started emptying out the coolers. The only options we had were, cook the food or throw it out. So, we would have smorgasbord for days. It was like a block party, minus the power. Thank God for a good ole Weber charcoal grill. And we weren't wanting for any options due to the variety of restaurants. (I think I gained ten pounds during Katrina)

After the food is eaten and the power restored, we all help to get each other back in business. It was a great little community family. We all did what we could, and soon everyone was back open. Downtown was up and running again.

Football

Football is huge here in Alabama. Everyone around the country knows the Alabama-Auburn rivalry. You have to pick a side, and our staff was split down the middle. Almost as popular is the loyalty to the New Orleans Saints. Mobilians are die-hard fans. Who Dat!

During football season, the staff could wear their football jerseys to work on Sundays. It was black and gold all over the restaurant. The Saints usually played the noon game, so it was always a fun time. In the main dining room, we had a projector and put up vinyl panels that covered the entire front of the restaurant. It was the biggest screen in town, like you were sitting on the sidelines, big as life. That was probably the best idea Byron ever had, and he couldn't care less about football. The customers would reserve their favorite tables in the dining room like they were booking seats at the Superdome.

I loved the Saints, but my team was the San Francisco 49ers. Duane was all about the Dallas Cowboys. We were the exceptions. We'd wear our own gear in the kitchen, the renegades.

Now fans have their superstitions, and they are very serious about them. We had one server who decided he could not wash his jersey when the Saints won. It would be bad luck. He would personally be responsible for the outcome if they lost the next game. That was fine and all until the year that the Saints had a huge winning streak—made it to the Superbowl. Now this server tended to sweat a lot anyway. Imagine what that jersey started to smell like. Okay, it's time to wash it or be off the schedule until January. He opted for the mini-vacation. Die-hard!

So, every Sunday, we were pretty much Who Dat Nation. Ella and Leah would come in decked out in their gear. Leah usually looked like she was auditioning for the Saintsations (the New Orleans Saints cheerleading squad) sporting some sort of sequined short shorts, ass hanging out (she had a nice ass) and boots. Ella came toting Franklin, a godawful rubber mask that she somehow decided was her good luck charm. When Leah was fortunate enough to not be put to work, those two were a sight at the bar. Now Ella was a tiny girl. Eighty pounds wet, but big things come in small packages. They sat next to this random guy at the bar one day, and Ella introduced herself sweetly. "Hello, I'm Ella, I'm about to be your biggest nightmare." Cute, he thought, this little thing? He bought them a round of drinks. So as the game proceeds and the Saints are down, she suddenly turns the crazy on. She's back and forth pacing and standing on her barstool yelling, "Kill him... Break his kneecaps!" She was screaming at the top of her lungs at the tv as if they could hear her on the sidelines. (Now the Saints had already been sanctioned for unnecessary roughness that season, maybe they did). That guy moved by halftime. One time someone thought it would be funny to hide Franklin. Ella went insane, searching the restaurant frantically screaming as if someone had just stolen her child. Needless to say, Franklin turned up before kickoff.

One season the 49ers made it to the playoffs. (The Saints had already been knocked out.) I was on vacation, so Toni and Leah actually wore my 49ers gear to work for me that day, the only time they donned any other team's gear. Katie did too, but it wasn't that big of a deal for her. She really couldn't care less about football, she was a basketball girl. Celtics. I think Duane got a little jealous, because she never wore his Dallas gear! The 49ers won that day, by the way. Thanks, girls.

Senior Bowl

Every January, Mobile is the host city for the Senior Bowl. This unique game features the best collegiate seniors on teams that represent the North and South. They are also the NFL top draft prospects. These teams are coached by two NFL coaching staffs. This is always a fun time of year. The week before the game, all the NFL coaches are in town watching the practices and scouting the future stars, but they rarely stay to watch the actual game. Being the caliber of restaurant we were, the coaches would always eat there at some point during their stay. My favorite Senior Bowl was when the coaches for the San Francisco 49ers came in to eat. They were coaching the South team that year. I was so excited.

So, they were there, and I was acting like the Queen of England herself was dining with us. As soon as we slowed down enough, I proceeded to go out and talk with them for a bit. I think they were a little surprised to meet a 49ers fan in the middle of Saints nation. One of them got my card and said he would send me something from the team. People always say that usually just to be nice, so imagine my surprise when a FedEx package came in that next week. In it was a handwritten note, thanking me for my hospitality and saying how wonderful the meal was. Go Niners. The note was sitting on top of this awesome pullover logo jacket. I loved it! Even though the majority of football season in Mobile averaged eighty degrees outside, I wore that heavy-ass jacket every game. Didn't even care that I was sweating my ass off. Football superstitions. At least I washed it.

Regulars

We were fortunate enough to have a restaurant with a regular clientele. They became part of the family. They loved to get involved and help out. They felt a sense of camaraderie. This was their place. We had a great crowd of regulars. Our happy hour crowd was awesome. Our Sunday crowd even better. Two of my absolute favorites were Chad and Sarah.

Chad sat in his spot at the end of the bar, always working on the daily crossword puzzle from our local paper. He'd always walk in through the kitchen, stopping to sample whatever we were making. The man could cook. He could have been a master chef. He had traveled all over the world, taking culinary classes whenever he could. He knew more about exotic spices than my whole kitchen combined. He even turned me on to my spice vendor. On Sundays, he'd always bring in a big cup of boiled peanuts and share them with the staff. He'd sit back and observe the happenings around him, often commenting on situations he felt I needed to be aware of since I was primarily in the kitchen. Everyone went to Chad for advice, including me. No matter what the situation, he always had some profound solution. Smart man.

He loved Amber, our bartender. They were the best of friends. He was a pseudo-grandfather to her daughter. If she was working, he was there. On Sundays, he would always be there about fifteen minutes before we opened. As the line was forming at the gate, he'd come through the kitchen and take his spot at the bar. One Sunday he was late, with no call. He didn't show until fifteen minutes after we opened. We wrote him up. He laughed and signed it.

Sarah was a happy hour girl. Early afternoon. She came in and drank her "champs" (champagne) as she proclaimed to be working. The bartender would sometimes leave while Sarah was there, literally, go to the store or something. "Sarah's got the bar." And I was fine with that. She knew all the regulars, what they drank, all the special orders. Shit, she could train a new bartender better than I could. And whenever we had a fill-in, God, I hoped she was there. If she wasn't, I'd call her in like she worked there. For all of this, she got her perks. She got the bottomless champagne deal every day, not just Sunday. We loved her.

The lunchtime girls were awesome. None of them worked. They were all married with children. They would meet at the restaurant around noon, dressed in their workout clothes. (I don't think any of them but one actually went to the gym) They'd order a salad of some sort, sip on champagne and talk about where they were going for their next vacation and what they were cooking their family for dinner. They loved to tell me about these elaborate meals they were preparing. I don't know if they wanted my amazement at their fine culinary skills or were just trying to one-up me. Either way, they were serious about it. They had to keep those hubbies happy. Around two they would leave to stop by the grocery and pick up the kids.

Then there were the men. Most of them owned their own companies, enabling them to knock off at three and finish their workday at the bar. We had lawyers who came in after court, calling to have their office finish their agenda for the day. Then there was the hospital staff, coming in still in their scrubs. Everyone had their own seat at the bar. We might as well have put their names on it. There were the occasional exceptions to this barstool boys' club. Only two of them had wives who were allowed to join the party. I don't know if these women realized how special they were. But they were cool so they could belly up in the bar without complaints from the men.

The other women primarily sat outside in the courtyard. They actually worked a full day so they wouldn't get there until around five. They'd sit out there sipping on chardonnay, gossiping about everything, bitching about their jobs and solving the world's problems. They were always dressed to the nines, sporting the latest fashions complete with fabulous shoes. I loved it when we didn't have an event on a Friday night, and I could get off around five and join them, sporting my tired-ass kitchen outfit and clogs. I'd always bring them some snacks to sop up some of that wine and keep the gossip rolling. They were the reason I knew way too much dirt about everyone else. Of course, they were flawless. They were a hoot. Loved them.

At any given time, any of these people would answer the phone, take reservations, explain the special of the day or give a brief synopsis of our banquet room and talk about all the fabulous parties they had attended there. They liked being involved. It was like employees that paid us, and they hardly ever called in sick. We embraced the regulars and were damn lucky to have them.

The Restaurant Next Door

We had been open a few years when the space next door was finally leased, and we had a new restaurant coming in. They were upscale Mexican/Spanish-style cuisine. The more, the merrier. We were excited. So, they get open and we with our Southern charm, politely offer to them that if they need anything, just let us know. I don't know how versed you are with Southern ways, but like anything, it's a courtesy. It's not to be taken literally, especially all the time. Next thing you know they were coming over just about every day needing to borrow something. At first, we started a list but gave up when we realized it would never get paid back. Garlic, half & half, butter, lemons, lettuce, onions, peppers... you name it. It was all things a restaurant should be amply stocked with. They would even come over to get ketchup (because they didn't use it in the restaurant) for their personal food.

Usually, it was Tina, this short little thing who was always bitching about something, rambling on and on to who knows who, about who knows what. We tended to tune her out. We'd hear her coming, talking on her phone, bitching, walking in the door, "Giiiiirl, hold on... We need some onions... Uh huh, I know that's right, hold on... no, more than that... for real? Okay, then," and out the door she went, still just a talkin'. She cracked us up. Then they got to the point where they quit ordering aprons for the kitchen. Who does that? So the entire staff came over and used ours. Our linen order went up to the point that I quit ordering aprons and just bought my staff their own. It was a hell of a lot cheaper. It was insane. I mean every day, it was something.

Finally, I realized that I could turn this situation to my advantage. One day our oven went out, and we had a huge banquet that night. Don't think

I didn't prance over there myself and said I needed their oven for two hours. I didn't really ask, just said. Now, we were starting to see a trade-off. After that, I borrowed their entire kitchen for a catering gig that we had to prep during brunch, which wasn't happening in our kitchen. They were closed and came up and gave me the keys. The chef even helped me prep.

Then there were the people. One night my dishwasher was a no-show, and we had a huge wedding. Byron was part of the wedding party and he was back in the dish hole with a trash bag over his suit trying to wash the dishes. At least he was doing something. I did actually feel sorry for him, so I pranced over and flat-out told them I needed their dishwasher for the night. I mean they only had a few tables, they could handle that. Mind you, he stayed clocked in on their payroll. I sent him back just before close. Then I finally just flat out stole Monty from them.

They never did get that "keep your restaurant stocked" thing down, and Tina was in and out every day. It became clear to me that for as much as they constantly borrowed from us, when payback came, I was going to borrow big—people, equipment, even the whole kitchen. It seemed to work itself out. They finally sold to some corporate restaurant, who actually kept things stocked. My kitchen borrowing days were sadly over. And I have to say, I missed Tina.

We'll Get by with a Little Help...

Kitchen staff is one of the most challenging areas of the whole restaurant. I mean these are people of their own breed. Who honestly wakes up and says: I want to work long hours, never have a weekend off, sweat my ass off in a hot, crammed room and not get paid shit for it? The upside is you get to play with knives and act a fool. It's a love, pure and simple. Of course, you have your good, bad, and just plain ugly. You spend a lot of time kissing a lot of toads before you find that semblance of a prince.

Over the years, I've pretty much seen it all. We had a pretty bad stint for a while. We went through countless people until we finally found one who was worth a shit. We weren't asking for miracles, just someone who will show up, has decent knife skills and can follow directions. Oh, we had some characters. We got to the point where we started our own 86 list on the inside of the cooler door. Every time we'd hire a new guy, his name would be added to the list. Then when he was fired, we'd scratch it out and put our nickname for him.

The Drunk... We thought we had lucked out with him. He had awesome knife skills, knew his way around the kitchen, could run the line, sauté, grill, and fry. He was a great match. We loved him for five days. Then he got a day off. Oh my God, Dr. Jekyll and Mr. Hyde. He apparently went on a binge once he left work that day. By the time he came back to work, he had been up partying for a good thirty-six hours. He was wasted! He had stumbled to work, almost got hit by a car and puked his guts up outside the kitchen door. (That was lovely on a hot, humid day)

Now I was all about the get-out-of-jail-free card. I mean everyone can have a bad day, situation, issue, or whatever. He cashed his in his first week. We sent him home, gave him a ride, told him to sleep it off, and we'd see him tomorrow. It wasn't a week later that he was doing shots behind the line and suddenly started swaying. He stumbled out of the kitchen, pissed in the mop sink, and passed out in the stockroom. Before we could address this, in walks our health inspector. Great timing. She walked around the restaurant with me, clipboard in hand, and goes into the stock room. I prayed that he had stumbled out the door and was somewhere passed out in the bushes, out of sight. Not so lucky. There he was, laid out on the chest freezer, puke all over the floor, reeking like alcohol. She wasn't impressed. I don't know how we even passed that day, but for the grace of the gods, we did. Not without some severe scolding. Yeah, our health standards are impeccable, minus the piss in the sink and the puke in the stockroom. Needless to say, that was it for him.

The Momma's Boy... This guy came in with his mother to apply with us. A little weird, but we thought maybe she was his ride or something. Other than that, he seemed normal enough, had decent experience, so we hired him. He worked a couple of shifts then his mother called in sick for him. Are we in high school? His mother. You can't pick up the phone and call your work yourself? Anyway, by the third day of his mother calling in we told her to tell him not to bother coming back in. The next day he showed up with bells on, miraculously cured of whatever ailed him and was ready to work. He walked into the kitchen, with his mom in tow, of course. Bye-bye.

Mr. Gung Ho... He showed up to work his first day in a Mighty Mouse t-shirt. "Here I come to save the day." He thought he knew everything. No matter how many times you tried to show him how to do something the way WE do it, he thought he could do everything better. He drove us all crazy. Erica was on the floor one shift waiting tables and put in an order for bruschetta. After his third attempt to make it the way we did it, she grabbed the plate and screamed: "It's not brain surgery. It's fucking bruschetta!" Slam, down goes the plate, shattered all over the floor. Then she went behind the line and made it herself. They all fired him the next shift when I wasn't there.

The Asshole... This guy was good. He knew his shit. Unfortunately, he thought he knew more than all of us. From day one I thought he was the answer. Everyone kept telling me what a dick he was, but I didn't see it. When I was there, he was spot-on and very polite. Apparently, when I was not, he turned into Hitler, yelling at the servers, telling them how stupid they were. He created an "us" and "them" atmosphere that was not what our kitchen was all about, and dictated to the kitchen the way he wanted things. It was not the personality type we wanted in our little family, but he got shit done, so I kept giving him the benefit of the doubt.

Then one day they decided to set him up. They told him I was out of town when in reality they knew I was coming in to pick up some specialty items for a friend's wedding shower. Cody was waiting for me out in the parking lot. He made me come in the dish hole and be quiet. We were in the middle of a rush, and this guy was in high gear, being a complete asshole to everyone. I was so disappointed. I could not believe how he was belittling my family. This was clearly not a match. I walked into the kitchen and told him he needed to go. He was shocked to see me, and didn't have anything to say. He packed up his knives and left. Three weeks later he actually called to ask me out, since I wasn't his boss anymore. Are you serious? Uh, let me think about this… no!

The Culinary Student… I finally hired a girl. I've always thought that kitchen bitches rock. This girl was enrolled at our local culinary school, and we got her through an intern program. I thought this was finally the one to break this bad string. The first night she started, Erica and I were working. As she comes into the kitchen, she proclaims, "I've never been in a real restaurant kitchen before. This is cool." Are you serious? Erica and I were taken aback. You're in culinary school, and you've never worked in a kitchen? This apparently was her first job. And this is the smallest kitchen on the planet. Well, we'll give her a shot. She can't be any worse than what we've been through.

We had a recipe book, so we started her out with simple tasks. Make the dressings, prep the vegetables… simple. She did a good job, at first. She had decent knife skills. We could work with this. She became enamored with Duane. Every time he turned around, she was right there, all up in his space. She was like lint, can't brush it off. She made a little chef with a red heart for him out of dough and baked it. He hated that thing. We would constantly hide it in his cooler where we knew he would find it, taping little dialog bubbles to it… "I love you, Duane."… "Duane, why did you throw me in the trash?"… "What is your special tonight, Duane?"… "I'll help you with ANYTHING"… It went on and on. Drove him crazy.

She told us that her specialty was pastry. Okay, we all hated doing the desserts, so we put her in charge. She did all right until she started going out on a limb baking all kinds of crap that was completely inedible. She made me a cake for my birthday. It was a castle. Looked beautiful, tasted like a sand castle. What did she use, cornmeal instead of flour? It was awful.

Back to the basic dressings and prep, she started adding random things to the recipes. Things that didn't even go together in any shape or form. Can you not just read the recipe and follow it? How hard is that? Consistency was not her strong point. We felt the need to put up with her until the internship was over, babysitting her the entire time. Finally, it ended, and we were able to let her go. She actually graduated and became a certified chef. God help the next place.

We went through them. It was like a roller coaster that never stopped.

This was the point where I decided to prance next door and hit up Monty. Why did I just not do this before? He was good, and we needed him. We were running out of space on the cooler door. So, I stole him. Fair and square and our kitchen was finally complete.

Terms

Restaurant lingo is important. We have to be able to know where everybody stands, literally for some of these, and get everyone on the same page. There are many terms, but I'm going to elaborate on these select few.

86... One of the most important terms to learn whether you're front or back of the house is 86. This is a common phrase used all over the country. I've heard it originated from a prestigious club in New York, where the bartenders would call to 86 a customer, meaning throw them out on the street. The club was on 86th Street, hence the term. Whether that is fact or not is not the point. The point is that it is a common term throughout the restaurant world. In a kitchen, it means quite simply you are out of that item. Easy enough.

My favorite story is when Gina, our lovely champagne fairy, decided she wanted to wait tables. She had become comfortable popping and pouring, so wanted to try her hand at serving. Now mind you, she had never waited tables before or even worked in a restaurant for that matter, but her personality was outstanding, and she had gotten to know the menu items, so why not? I've been there myself. We decided to start her on a Friday night. This particular Friday was extremely busy. We had a rehearsal dinner, booked dining room and courtyard. It was the perfect time to get her feet wet. Erica got the specials board ready for the night and adds "86 lamb". The first table Gina gets is a twelve top from out of town wanting that true "fine-dining" experience. Little Miss Fairy Dust is not exactly the perfect fit, but we didn't have too much of a choice. It is what it is. She does a fantastic job describing the menu, upsells the wine and courses the meal (appetizers, salad, entrée, dessert). For those of you unfamiliar with restaurants, this is the perfect ticket, all four courses sold. She apparently described the lamb to perfection, eight of them ordered it. She couldn't have been more proud.

Erica got the ticket and immediately screamed for Gina. She came in the kitchen grinning from ear to ear, so proud of her very first and perfect ticket table. Now Erica is a screamer behind the line, she's even been known to throw a plate of food on the floor if it's not made right. But this is her best friend, and Gina is just so bubbly and nice, it's almost impossible to get mad at her. So Erica, scarily but very calmly asked Gina if she read the special board. Gina (still smiling ear to ear) nodded her head. Erica asked, still calm, "Did you see where it said 86 lamb?" Gina nodded and smiled even bigger. Erica now paused and took a deep breath, "Do you know what 86 means?" Gina started to nod as she uttered, "yeeeees," then started shaking her head "noooooo." Erica had held it together as long as possible. She screamed, "It means we don't fucking have any!" Now, this just about brought Gina to full-on tears. The grin was gone, and there was a tear forming. She really was so proud of herself thinking that we had eighty-six orders of lamb to sell and she had just sold eight of them.

I mean, if you think about it, who has eighty-six orders of anything to sell? And if you have that many, you damn sure don't need to put it on the specials board. That board is reserved for when you get low on an item, or only have so many specials to sell. Gina just got schooled in Restaurant 101. I guarantee she won't ever forget that term. She didn't wait tables much longer after that. I think she was a little scared of Erica yelling at her again.

Heard... One of the most important terms in the kitchen. It simply means to acknowledge what has just been said. But it can't be taken lightly. When you need four steaks fired (start cooking now), or you need three wontons dropped (put in the fryer), the said person on that station needs to give you a heard. That assures you that said task is being done. When the sauté chef says he's firing three alfredos, he needs a heard from the person running the line. It's quite simple really, but extremely important.

Now beware of the fake heard, or the heard and forgot. You know the saying, in one ear and out the other. That is never going to be a good situation when it comes time to plate that dish, and one component hasn't even been fired yet. Now some people can take this to the extremes, causing there to be a love/hate relationship with this word, but in general, it needs to be acknowledged. It makes for a much smoother night.

This is equally important when communicating with the servers. If you 86 an item, you need a heard from one of them, assuring you that it will be passed along to everybody else (or so you hope). I once had a new server that stood there mindlessly as I 86-ed the fish special one night. Can I get a heard? Again, can I get a heard? He finally looked at me and said, I heard you, I just don't know what that means. Okay back to basics with this one. 86. We've sold out of the fish. Don't order any more.

Behind... This acknowledges where a said person is in relation to you. Very important when they have a hot pan, behind... hot. Or a sharp knife, behind... sharp. This lets people know to move, or not move and stay out of the way. Our kitchen was so small that this was almost overused. Monty was the worst. Whenever he felt like getting through, he'd proclaim, "Behind hot... sharp," and waltz through the kitchen. Usually, he had nothing in his hand, but you still had to be aware and move. We had a new girl in the kitchen one night, and she was working with me on the line. She neglected to say, "Behind... hot," as she was putting a spitting hot grease-laden pan in the bus tub on the floor. Next thing you knew I turned, knocked it and the grease went all down my leg into my shoe. I've never moved so fast. I flung my shoe, thank God for kitchen clogs, ripped my sock off and immediately doused my foot under cold water in the sink. Still have a scar from that one.

Throughout these stories you will hear other terms which I will quickly describe:

All Day... The total count of an item based on the tickets currently hanging on the line

Covers... This refers to the number of people, one person, one cover.

Dying... When food has been plated and sat too long in the window waiting for the server. It is getting to the point of unservable. The person expediting uses this quite a bit.

Fire... That means start cooking said item now. Also referred to as drop, depending on the equipment used to cook said item. Note: For the front of the house that is the button they push on their order screen that sends it back to the kitchen.

In the Weeds... When you have so many orders at one time, the kitchen has become chaotic. Also referred to as drowning, going down in flames, buried or just plain fucked. It's an adrenaline rush for sure.

On the Fly... Someone messed up, either it wasn't rung, it's a recook, or simply forgotten. Either way, it means yesterday, get it out as fast as you fucking can.

Runner... Someone, anyone who takes food that is on the verge of dying to the table before it does. Usually not the server that put the order in.

Singled Out... This is an item on a ticket all by itself. Can be fired when convenient, it doesn't go with anything else.

Walking In... This is a new ticket that has just rung into the kitchen, not included in the last all day counts

Window... The shelf where plated food is set awaiting the server to pick it up. Usually has heat lamps to keep it warm.

The Expeditor... The single most important job in the kitchen. This is the person in charge of getting the food called and plated. Quite simply, they maintain the flow of the kitchen. This person can also have you in the weeds in two seconds if the tickets are not called right. There is no one formula for expediting. A good one needs to adapt to everyone's ways in the kitchen. Organization is the most important skill to have. They don't necessarily need to know how to cook, just the timing of the process. Some of the best expeditors I've had were not cooks, but they were excellent organizers. Time management is key! You are responsible for ensuring five different items with four different cook times come out at the same time.

Each item needs to be called to said station at the right time to make this happen. Otherwise, food sits dying in the window waiting on all the items to get ready.

The communication must flow between the expeditor and the rest of the kitchen. Heard is extremely important. You can tell the grill person to fire four filets all day, but if they didn't hear it, it ain't happening. Typically, your back is turned, so you don't even know until you go to plate it that it hasn't even been fired yet. Once heard has been established, keep communicating. Always double check about halfway between calling said item and actually needing it. That is the point where if the heard and forgotten has happened, they can fire it on the fly. This will still get it to you on time.

CH. 3
SUNDAY FUNDAY

AFTER WE BOUGHT THE RESTAURANT, we started Sunday brunch. We quickly became THE brunch spot in Mobile. We did it right. It was a fixed price with about a dozen entrée selections. Every plate came with bread pudding, a scoop of grits or country fried potatoes, a biscuit or English muffin and two eggs cooked to order. We had a Bloody Mary bar with all the fixin's, bottomless champagne and a "champangel" to serve it, live jam music, an awesome courtyard, bar, and two dining rooms. We sat about three hundred people at full capacity, and after a few months, were always on a wait.

The whole crew loved working Sundays, a rarity in most restaurants. It was the one day the whole family worked together. We were so busy we even had a crew of people who only worked on Sundays. The servers made a shit-ton of money, and the kitchen crew loved the adrenaline rush, pumping out all those orders. It was our fun day. There were a handful of servers who would rotate into the kitchen and help expedite the line. They would get all the orders on trays with appropriate condiments ready for the servers to pick it up and go. Cody had hired all the boys, backservers, and they were their own little cult crew. Good boys. They worked their asses off, keeping everything iced down, running food, bringing waters and bussing tables. We were a solid crew.

The kitchen came in first. We had a specific order we used to prep for the day and had it down to a science. We had to. Our kitchen was the size of a walk-in closet, so order was important. Brown the butter for the hollandaise, make the bread pudding, cook off the bacon, biscuits, grillade sauce, slice the prime rib and steaks. Once this was in the works, we would focus on the daily specials, fish sauce, frittata fixin's and whatever we were running as a special that day.

When one person was late, it threw a wrench into our routine. Hence, we started the rule if you're more than thirty minutes late, you're cleaning the kitchen by yourself. This was the best rule we ever set. Paco was cleaning solo at least twice a month. And that little kitchen looked like a tornado had just barreled through it by the end of brunch. Starting with the three cases of broken egg shells behind the sauté station, through to the line. Shit was everywhere. Even if it was a full crew cleaning, we sat out back for about thirty minutes at the end of the shift, popped a bottle of champagne and smoked our cigarettes getting mentally geared up to walk back into that war zone and make it look like a kitchen again. Most bosses would frown on that, but I was part of the crew, so I knew we needed that break. Of course, we looked like a motley crew with remnants of brunch plastered all over us. I always had dried hollandaise in my hair. We were a sight.

Paco and I ran the line. I pulled the tickets and made the calls, he set up the plates. Monty was the grill man, sandwiched between the oven and the grill. He and Paco ran the oven. Duane was on sauté, flipping all the eggs to order and running the fryer, passing off everything to Paco. Cody helped with whatever station needed him while humping everything in the kitchen. Paco was the only one who was mobile. I was crammed in by the wall, and my right foot never moved. I was in charge of the egg calls.

The timing here was important. Eggs had a short cooked lifetime. Too early and they'd get cold. Too late and the food died on the line under the heat lamps waiting for them. Brunch food had to move, and move fast, to get to the tables. No one wants cold eggs. Hence the rotating servers, or as we so lovingly referred to them, kitchen bitches. They kept that food flowing and the other servers in check. When you only have a dozen items on the menu, every server decides that that chicken and waffle and lobster crêpes in the window must be theirs. I got so tired of screaming not to pull anything out of the window without a ticket that I nipped the problem in the bud… kitchen bitches.

Of course, for all the planning, organization, and timing, we still had glitches. It's amazing how it only takes one curveball to throw the kitchen underwater. Once we were plating a twenty top in the middle of a mad rush. We needed to move and move fast, as we only had room to hold eleven plates under the heat lamps at a time. Byron had decided to come visit with us in the kitchen in the middle of this craziness, since apparently, he could find nothing to do to help out. He was rambling on about some story that we are not even listening to. I was slamming out round two for this table, and I'm missing a plate. "Where's the frittata?" I look up and there he is, a piece of frittata in hand chewing on the bite he'd just taken. Are you kidding me? You're eating the frittata? So I call for one on the fly, which is still going to take a good ten minutes. I was pissed. I told him to go out to the table, which now has food except for the frittata guy, and explain to the person that ordered it that you ate his frittata... sorry... and tell him how good it was while you're at it. If you don't, I damn sure will. My kitchen was spot-on.

When Fynn came on board, we had just created a Chicken Bitch station across the kitchen. He was in charge of chicky, chicky, wawas. (Chicken and waffles). We had a little baby home fryer and a waffle iron over there, and yes, it kept him busy as shit all day. That took a huge burden off the main fryer, and we finally had one seafood-free fryer option.

In the beginning, the bottomless "champagne" was free with brunch. We eventually started charging for it and periodically crept up the price. Nobody seemed to care. We'd go through around thirty to forty cases of Cook's every Sunday. With that kind of alcohol consumption, nothing shocked us. There was all kinds of crazy. Most of our customers were drinking professionals. Occasionally someone would try to keep up with them, and it usually ended with them being carried out of the restaurant, or in one case being dragged out on the floor mat.

It took a hot minute to streamline brunch. At first, we offered choices, grits or potatoes, and biscuit or English muffin. The kitchen had to decipher these tickets to plate them correctly, and this took some time. It was fine until we had our first packed brunch, the first time we had the whole restaurant booked solid. It was Mother's Day and our local college's graduation the same day.

Now I had strategically planned the reservations and blocked out a thirty-minute time slot to serve the graduation reservations before we resumed regular seating. Everything was going to be so smooth. Not! The college's graduation lasted forty-five minutes longer than it was supposed to.

We served the early regular reservations, and we waited… and waited. We went out back to smoke cigarettes, and the boys started shooting hoops… waiting. Where the hell are these people? Thirty minutes of nothing to do. Then the floodgates opened.

The graduation reservations finally showed up right when the late reservations started seating. Oh yes, this was happening, the whole restaurant was seating at once. And we were not prepared for that. That ticket machine started going off and never stopped. They were hanging on the floor, out the door, around the corner, down the street… Okay, here we go. Jump straight into the deep end and hold your breath. We're going to sit at the bottom for a while.

People were starving, especially the graduation crowd. They had already endured an extended ceremony and were ready to eat. Well, that just wasn't happening. My family attended my brother-in-law's graduation that day and were part of that crowd. I was running around making cheese and cracker plates for the tables just to get them something to snack on. The kitchen typically closed at three o'clock, but we were still cooking food until almost five! Two hours plus cook times. Oh my God, it was a nightmare! My poor family got there at two fifteen, didn't get food till four forty-five. Are you out back waiting for the chicken to lay the eggs? I couldn't even get food to my family. So much for knowing the owner.

After that day, we streamlined. Every plate got a scoop of grits and potatoes, both, no more choices. And we put the biscuit or English muffin choice on the servers. All we had to do was eggs and entrées. It doesn't sound like a big deal, but it made a huge difference in plating times. It set us up for the volume we were about to consistently do in the future. We were ready. Bring it… And they did.

The First Record-Breaking Brunch

So, we hit a standstill with our brunch. We always did just under $5000 but could not break that figure to save our lives. It went on for months. One Sunday, as we were about to close, yet again about $100 shy of the $5000 mark, one of our regulars had a grand idea. If all the girls flashed their tits, he would spend $100 on a drink. Now if he was willing to fork out that kind of money, why not just buy the bar a round and be done with it. No, he wanted titties. We discussed it. Yes, to my crew this wasn't a far-fetched idea. We decided, what the hell. I mean we all had nice tits, and it's not like we haven't flashed them in bars in front of complete strangers before, or better yet at Mardi Gras parades to get the big beads.

It was only the staff and a few regulars left in the bar at this time. Now there were rules. First, he decided that no other men would be in the room when said flashing occurred. The kitchen staff wasn't too thrilled about that one, but as he laid the hundred-dollar bill on the bar, he said, "My money, my rules." Okay, next we were all to sit at the bar and flash him one by one, not all at one time. He wanted to drag it out as long as possible, getting the most bang for his buck. We sat down, and everyone with a penis left the room, except Kameron. He didn't count. He couldn't care less about titties. It was settled that he acted as the referee. You could hear the kitchen boys bitching from around the corner, claiming how unfair this was, but they were his rules. There were eight of us, all of the female employees, except Marleena. She pretended to not understand, and two of our regular customers. They loved the idea of helping out the team, made them feel like part of the crew, besides they had a pretty good buzz by this time. More titties for him. Kameron started the countdown, and the flashing commenced. In the end, he not only honored his hundred dollars (actually $102.75), he bought all of us a drink, adding another sixty bucks to the tab. Then we popped a bottle of champagne and passed it around, men included, to celebrate finally breaking the five-thousand-dollar mark.

It took a hot minute to break this record, but once we did, $5000 was a thing of the past. We more than doubled that figure most Sundays when we finally maxed out seating capacity, but we will never forget that first record-breaking brunch and the titty—I mean team—effort it took to get there. Love my girls.

The Pajama Party

We had finally broken our $5000 mark but were still hanging at that plateau. Our favorite local radio station broadcasted a Sunday Jazz Brunch show every week. It was hosted by one of our celebrity DJs, Catt. We weren't really a jazz venue, but the owner of the station was one of our regulars, and we made a deal with him to broadcast the show live from our courtyard one Sunday. It was set. Byron decided we needed to have a pajama party that day. "The Cat's Pajamas." Awesome idea, by the way. We advertised the party and made sure all our regulars knew.

The entire staff showed up in whatever their version of pajamas was. (No, they didn't show up nude). Ava really did look like a Victoria's Secret model that day. Paco just had to show up. He always wore his PJs anyway. Amber sported a cute little ruffled nightie complete with hair bows and a teddy bear. Marleena wore this beautiful silk pajama pantsuit. I opted for the sporty look with a racer back and striped PJ pants which would go with my pink kitchen clogs. Catt arrived to get set-up dressed like Hugh Hefner, donning a smoking jacket, slippers, and pipe. It was awesome. Everyone was in the swing of the PJ party.

The customers started to arrive, and we were amazed how many of them were dressed in their pajamas. Sarah and her crew came in wearing their men's button-down shirts, completing the look with bed-head hair. Chad actually bought some Spiderman Underoos and brought them, didn't wear them. He was in theme in his smoking jacket, too. Some people were a little leery about the pajama thing. They came in regular clothes and when they saw everyone else dressed (or not dressed) went to change. By midway through brunch, almost the entire restaurant looked like they were having a lounging party at home. I felt bad for the few customers that didn't get wind of this. They felt so out of place.

Catt broadcast through brunch that day and brought in a crowd that had never been there before. This was the plateau breaker we needed. We built a whole new clientele that day who became part of the regulars. We almost doubled our record, all without titties. It just kept getting better.

The Fire

One Sunday we had a fire. It started in the girls' bathroom, in the ceiling vent. Amber went into pee and came running out, screaming "The bathroom's on fire!" She ran behind the bar to grab the fire extinguisher, which was currently a purse rack. Only about twenty purses were hanging on it. As she's frantically throwing purses across the bar, she grabbed my left tit. "Momma the bathroom's on fire!" Somehow holding my tit was comforting her. Before she got to the bottom of the stack, the fire truck was there. We were literally down the block from the fire department. You could see it from our front gate. They came in, evacuated the building, and went to work.

Of course, we were busy as shit, right in the middle of brunch. All the customers got up grabbed their purses and champagne and went outside. Suddenly we had the biggest street party in town. No one left. There were literally about two hundred people in the streets, all drinking champagne. It was like Mardi Gras. When the champagne got low, they started asking Ava for refills. Okay, this is Mobile, so Ava and I went in and dragged one of the big white ice chests full of champagne out and started popping bottles. She mentioned that she should get hazard pay for going into a "burning building" to keep the customers happy. The champagne kept flowing, the party kept going. Everyone was taking selfies hanging off the fire truck, and with the firemen as they came and went. They were having a blast.

We were finally cleared to let everyone back in the building. They sat down and asked when their food would be ready. Seriously?... Only in Mobile. The kitchen had been shut down by the fire department. All the equipment was cold. We cranked the kitchen back up and had all the servers reorder food for the people still there. It took a hot minute, but we managed to get it all out. Don't even think about bitching about cook times, not today! Literally, only two tables left when the building was evacuated. Everyone else stayed. What's a little fire?... It's brunch.

Joe Cain

Joe Cain Day brunch was almost as big as Mother's Day. We were booked solid for weeks in advance. This was the start of the final days of Mardi Gras. The final hurrah. The procession started early in the morning.

It was the "people's parade." You didn't have to belong to any mystic society, didn't have to follow a theme, didn't have to wear a specific costume, you just had to organize some sort of float and sign up. There was also a walking parade that followed the floats. It was nonstop all day long.

There was no option of being off on Joe Cain. Everyone was on staff, no exceptions. Toni and Kameron always marched with the Dauphin Street Drunks in the procession that day, and they still came to work. They would show up just before we opened after loading all their gear, decked out in their pirate gear. They waited on one table. We had a table of travel writers who came to eat every Joe Cain Day before they headed downtown to cover all the festivities. This table was organized by our Convention and Visitors Bureau. It was a different group of writers from all over the country each year. The writers loved the fact that the pirates were their servers. It didn't hurt that we were written up in local papers all over the country. Toni and Kameron would surprise the writers with pirate gear and invite them to march with them. They were never turned down. It started their coverage with a bang. After that table, off they went, writers in tow. Arrrr.

We had to hire security for the door every Joe Cain Day. This was largely due to the bathroom situation, and to keep some sort of order. If you didn't have a reservation, you weren't getting in. It was like a private party that was invitation only. We were the hottest ticket in town. Start your day with some great food and champagne or the Bloody Mary bar, for those needing a little hair of the dog. We had such a great clientele, including the standing reservation of the Red Hat Society every year. Loved those ladies! Most people were decked out in all kinds of tacky. That's just what it was all about. And don't forget the beads. The more, the merrier.

If It's Broke

Equipment is a huge part of any restaurant. It's inevitable that equipment will go on the blink, and probable that it will be at the worst possible time. In hindsight, I wish I had gone to refrigeration repair school and electronic repair classes. Oh my God, the thousands of dollars I would have saved on repairs. Especially since labor is over half the cost.

The worst possible time is not even an exaggeration. One year, during Mardi Gras, the Saturday night before Joe Cain Day, our fryer decided to go out. Seriously? Right now? Fixing it was not an option. It was a necessity. So, I call the service company. Yes, I know it's a weekend... extra service call fee... Yes, I know it's Mardi Gras (considered holiday time in this city)... another extra fee... Oh, and we are in the middle of the parade route circle... pain-in-the-ass extra fee just to show up. $350 later, I am left with no choice. No way we are getting through Joe Cain brunch with no fryer. So, I agree and painstakingly explain to the driver how to get to us in the middle of the parades, as most of the streets are blocked off. I also give him the make and model number of the fryer and tell him exactly what is going on with it.

We wait and wait. It's been two hours since we called. He should be here by now. Finally, we get a call from him. He's stuck. He can't cross Broad Street because of the parade. Duh! I told you how to avoid that and go the roundabout way to get here. What an idiot! He clearly could not understand my directions, so he waited until the parade has passed, and the roads had opened. It's now almost ten o'clock. His hourly rate started when he got stuck at the parade, so I'm already into a little over an hour of labor on top of the exorbitant service call fee.

When he finally gets there, he tinkers with it and tells us what's wrong, but doesn't have the right part on his van to fix it. He tells us he has to go back to the shop. I was about to crawl out of my skin! He knew what he was coming to do. I gave him all the information about this fryer and what it was doing. Why would he not have the parts? He acted, or hoped maybe, that we would just say forget about it. No, we need this fryer. We'll wait. It takes another hour or so for him to return, finally, with the part he needs. Yes, all the time he's still on the clock. Another hour later the fryer is fixed. Fixed to the tune of $880! (By the way, the actual part was eighty dollars.) I could have almost bought a brand-new fryer for that! But what do you do? This was like a hostage situation. Pay, or it will be dead. Why can't these things happen on a Tuesday afternoon?

When It Rains

Again, in the middle of brunch—can't ANYTHING break on a Tuesday? It's raining. Let me just explain—it's a beautiful sunny day outside. There's not a cloud in the sky, and the courtyard is packed. It's raining in the kitchen, and I mean raining! The water pipes in the ceiling had burst. We were trying to roll along rigging up all kinds of shit to keep the water off the food. It was like Chinese water torture, as both our hands were pretty much occupied. We needed those little beanie caps, you know the ones with the little umbrellas on them. It's the worst nightmare for a kitchen.

I was so frustrated. I went out to the bar to get the boys a shot. It was the least I could do, as they were not complaining. No, they were prancing around singing in the rain… literally, the song, trying to make light of the situation. I got to the bar and laughingly asked, "Is there a plumber in the house?"

At that moment there was a voice from the bar, "I'm a plumber." It was like an angel, a knight in shining armor, sitting right there in front of me. "What have you got?" Seriously, come with me. He walked back to the kitchen with me and just stared at the situation in awe. "Y'all have a serious problem." Really? Tell me something I don't know.

We knew this situation was coming but had been quoted almost $4000 to fix it. That's a lot of money to shell out when it wasn't quite broken yet. He crawled up in the attic, assessed the problem, and told us exactly what it would take to fix it then quoted us half the price. He also separated it into two jobs, prioritizing the most important. Done. He was there the next day to complete step one. When he pulled the pipe out, he showed us all the splices that had been made on just one line. There were twelve in one five-foot section! I mean the plumbers we had been calling were just fixing the immediate leak to the tune of sixty-five dollars a pop knowing it would burst again in two weeks. They were also the ones who had quoted us $4000 to fix it. Twelve times sixty-five dollars… you do the math. They were robbing us.

It was so nice to find an honest plumber who did shit right. Did I mention he was my angel? He was a treasured unicorn, a rarity. He never paid for a brunch again.

Free Your Coon

The only wedding reception we ever did on a Sunday was doomed from the get-go. First, we only had two hours to clear everyone out and set the whole place back up for the event. To this day I still don't know what I was thinking. During brunch, we suddenly had an issue. This couple had come in dressed to the nines in their seersucker suit and floppy hat. They proceed to take to the Bloody bar and the champagne. In the meantime, they had left a cage in the back of their truck with a raccoon (coon, as we call it in the South) in it. They intended to free it across the bay after brunch. Now Amber was a die-hard save-the-world girl, and as she went out back for a quick smoke break, she saw this cage in their truck. It was a hundred degrees outside, and this coon didn't even have water. She goes on a rampage about saving this thing. Leah was "working" that day and of course, jumped right on the bandwagon with her.

We were starting to get busy. I vaguely remember looking up and seeing them rummage through the utensil bin and grabbing a turkey baster. I didn't think much about it at the time, but oh my God. They were out there trying to drip water in the coon's mouth with this baster. (Not a brilliant plan by the way). The coon just wasn't cooperating. Finally they approached the couple and explained their dilemma. The couple couldn't care less and just blew them off. They were more concerned about where the champangel was. They settled on throwing ice cubes into the cage. Still, it was so hot outside, and the poor thing was miserable. Brunch went on, and the champagne was flowing for this couple. We get the last orders out and call it. Time to revamp the kitchen and get this wedding out. Little did I know, that wasn't even close to happening.

We're balls-to-the-wall pumping out this food, right on schedule. I got to a break and went to check on the restaurant to see if I could help with the set-up. The place was trashed. Where were my servers? Nothing has even been done yet, and we only have an hour or so before the reception starts. WTF? I went out back, and there was my staff. Amber and Leah have accosted this couple. The girl, who had a good buzz going at this point, had kicked her heels off, and was threatening to kick their asses, all while wearing her big floppy hat.

Leah had called the animal rights people who were now on their way to get the coon. They would not let this couple leave until they got there. The whole front of the house staff was blocking their way to the truck. It was like a goddamn riot situation.

The police had apparently been called and were trying to sort out this whole mess. One thing was sure—they were not letting these people even think about driving. They had already told them if they got in their truck, they'd have a DUI before they left the parking lot. At this point, the local news and newspaper reporters have shown up and were interviewing the gang about animal rights issues and such. It was a scene. This coon has now reached celebrity status.

People! We have a wedding to set up. Are you serious right now? The only person inside doing anything to set up was Lukas, who didn't give a shit about the coon. He would have solved that problem before it got caged, kill it and boil it up… Good eating.

The whole situation was getting insane. Meantime Lukas had set up the cake. It was an elaborate three-tier work of art. He put it on the hostess stand which we positioned front and center as the guests walked in the door. I went back outside to see if maybe I can get my staff to come back in and pretend to be working. Now the news, the animal rights activists, the animal control people, my staff and this couple are all in a screaming match. Oh my God, we have thirty minutes until the wedding shows up, guys! Hello!

I go back inside and Lukas has the big eyes. That's what he does when there is a problem. The people upstairs had apparently taken a shower, and the ceiling was leaking… Right on the wedding cake! I go get Duane. He's the pastry man. If anyone can half-ass fix it, he can. He starts moving fondant flowers around and "gluing" them to the drip spots. This was really becoming my biggest nightmare.

Finally, my staff freed this coon (and hopefully not killed the couple), but at this point, I didn't really care. They came back in the restaurant, ready to get this wedding together. Thanks for joining us, guys. Let's spend this last fifteen minutes wisely. They started scrambling around and we somehow got the place in check. We had to move the cake against the wall to disguise the back part and the half-ass patch job we did to disguise the water leak. The wedding party arrived and raved about how perfect everything was, never even noticed the cake. Thank God… they don't even know! It amazed me that we managed to pull this off. Coon or no coon, we never booked a Sunday evening event again.

Hot Mess

Brunch was always fun for the kitchen. It was one of those shifts that was a constant adrenaline rush. We did what we could to make it our Sunday Funday. Like I said, I was fortunate enough to have a crew that loved their Sundays. By the end of the day, we were spent. The kitchen looked like a tornado had plowed through it. The boys would act a little crazy. Too many times Cody would take the leftover poached eggs and start hurling them at us through the parking lot. Once he even drank the egg water on a dare. Disgusting! On any given Sunday, they would shake up the champagne and spew it all over everyone. We usually closed that shift looking (and smelling) like a hot mess. It looked like we had just trudged through a war zone.

During football season, the boys always had some ridiculous bet going on and showed up in God knows what when they lost. Once Duane, Cody, and Paco showed up wearing pink bras over their shirts and tutus. Halfway through the shift, Duane threw it across the kitchen screaming, "I can't work in this bra!" Really? How do you think I feel? Another time it was cocktail dresses they had scored at Goodwill. Why did it always seem to involve women's clothing? And they gave Fynn a hard time!

After cleaning, we usually met up at our local watering hole. They did free crawfish on Sunday nights. We'd get there about when the first batch was ready. The regulars there knew we'd show and would leave us our "spot" at the end of the bar. I would like to say they were being nice, but in reality, they probably just didn't want to smell us. It was time to chill, suck the heads (because that is the proper way to eat crawfish) and down some much-needed shots. Thank God we were closed on Mondays.

Just Breathe

We were generally a well-oiled machine in the kitchen. But there were days when I knew we were fucked before the shift even began. You're a man down, and you know there is no way the line is going to go smooth. These are the nights where you might as well all hold hands and jump into the deep end, straight to the bottom of the pool. You're going to spend half your night drowning down there anyway. You just keep going, knowing that eventually, you hope, you will get to the surface to tread water and breathe. I know that sounds a little dramatic, but for real, when you are a man down, that means that some station is not covered. Everyone else is scrambling around trying to do their own station, and half-ass trying to cover the empty one. It's nothing but chaos from the first ticket to the last. And never fail, the restaurant is overbooked and never stops. This is when the extra adrenaline rush kicks in. You jump into a gear that you didn't realize existed while you hold your breath and hope for the best. You push out food as fast as you physically can in some haphazard order knowing that eventually, when the tickets stop, you might get a breath.

It's brunch, and as usual, we are guaranteed to be balls-to-the-wall busy. Always busier than our little kitchen should be able to handle. But somehow, we always did it. This is primarily because despite our kitchen size we had honed what we liked to call, the kitchen dance.

Now in most kitchens that entailed some sort of movement across the kitchen, randomly making that turn to pass. In ours, it meant planting one foot and pivoting. There was no place to move, no place to go. We had a well-oiled assembly line, each item was passed down until it reached the person plating it. If anyone had to move the planted foot, cook times would suffer. The only one who had the freedom to dance with everyone was Paco. When we really got balls-to-the-wall busy, we'd put on our kitchen song, "Get Lucky" by Daft Punk. It was the perfect rhythm for the kitchen dance. Kitchen people, listen to it. You'll see.

Man Down

Well when you have a man down, that requires everyone to have to move both feet. Suddenly our well-executed waltz turned into an awkward teenage middle school dance move. The choreography is fucked, and we all bumble around. This is when kitchen accidents happen: things get dropped, people get burned. It's not a graceful scene. So, a man down Sunday, and we're fucked. Paco is a no-show. We had already set up his station. We were used to that because he was always late. And thirty minutes late meant we were all off kitchen-cleaning duty and he, once again, would be doing it solo. We were totally down with that. But as the time ticked by, we realized he was beyond late, and not answering his phone. He had one of those pay-as-you-go plans, and it never seemed to be loaded.

I was genuinely concerned. This was totally out of character for him. Regardless, we were a man down, and because he was my partner in crime on Sundays, plating and calling the line, this affected me particularly. He made the oven and grill calls to Monty, and I would call to Duane on sauté and fry, primarily the egg calls. We'd typically go through thirty dozen plus eggs a day since every plate came with two eggs made to order. Now, I was flying solo... Shit! That meant that I had to talk to the servers too. Marleena! We spent the day scrambling, pretty much fucked from the get-go. Usually I was crammed in the corner behind the line, barely able to move, much less pivot. Today I was dancing all over the kitchen... Okay, two steps, but still, two steps too many.

It was the usual chaos, then added chaos on top of chaos. With a man down, the team had completely lost their rhythm. Monty was trying to help me plate, without even knowing what it's supposed to look like. He was the grill man. Temp a steak, no problem. Make it look pretty on a plate, what? Cody was running the oven all up in Monty's way. Both of them half-ass trying to do Paco's dance moves and bitching the whole time. Monty put on some godawful "kill... kill... kill" music, which I was barely tuning out at this point. Duane was flipping eggs six burners at a time, trying to help the grill and work the fry. He's throwing grit cakes across the kitchen for Fynn to put in his chicken fryer (impressive that Fynn caught most of them). Suddenly the worst thing imaginable happens. The kitchen printer went down!

Granted, this would never happen with a full crew. It's like the printer knew and just wanted to fuck with us. The servers had to start handwriting their tickets. With nine servers, the first ten minutes were spent trying to figure out which tickets actually fired to the kitchen and which we didn't have already. Of course for good measure, they went ahead and wrote their outstanding orders anyway, even though we had already established which ones we did have. We plated a lot of double orders that day. (At least the staff ate well) Getting them to write said tickets with our kitchen codes was like pulling teeth. We had a system for this, a list of all the menu items and their proper abbreviations for the kitchen tickets which they should have known. Should being the key word here. All their training was suddenly forgotten in the middle of this chaos. The servers were writing us novels for tickets. Behind the line the less reading we have to do, the quicker we were going to get out the food.

Then there was the handwriting factor. I swear since this technology age kids learn to text before they learn how to speak. Do they even teach kids to write in school anymore? I guess I'm old-school, I had to spend hours and hours learning to write properly. I don't even know if that is required anymore. Anyway, their handwriting is horrible! And oh, Marleena. She could barely speak English, much less write it. For most of hers I'd just call for her, ask what she wanted, and write up the ticket myself, which was exactly what I wanted to do when we were this busy, and this behind... have a fucking conversation with a server. My motto behind the line was don't talk to me. I've got a swarm of organized information in my head and don't have time to listen to or hear anyone but Paco. I had a knack for tuning people out. Talk to Paco. They knew the drill. He'd either solve the issue or pass any relevant information on to me, and he could speak Spanish to Marleena. But Paco wasn't there.

That day was a kitchen nightmare. I would have liked to see Gordon Ramsey handle that one. I'm sure the f-word would have been used twice as much. We somehow muddled through it. Eventually breaking through the water, breathing once again. Finally, it was over. We sat out back for a hot minute, realizing that we all had to clean the kitchen, and psyching ourselves up for it. After smoking a half a pack of cigarettes, and a good bottle and a half of champagne, we went into the war zone. Oh, Paco was going to pay for this one! Then five minutes later, he shows, with nothing but a, "Sorry guys. I've got this," and starts cleaning. We never asked him what was up, frankly didn't care at this point. We all went back outside, popped another bottle, and never even felt bad. He had redeemed himself. I didn't even cash in his get-out-of-jail-free card.

Lightning Strikes

Okay, it was another packed out, crazy day. It was storming outside, so we were minus the courtyard, trying to cram everyone into the dining and banquet room areas. Tables were on top of tables. Our table numbering system was out the window. The servers were breaking out the white fold-out banquet tables, putting them wherever they could and covering them with tablecloths. It was madhouse for out front. The kitchen was running smooth, dancing our dance and pumping out the orders. We felt their pain, though we're breathing and thankful this time it wasn't us... Oh wait, I forgot to knock on wood.

A huge bolt of lightning flashed, lit up the whole sky. Then not a second later—boom! The roar of thunder was so loud it was ear shattering. Our power flickered, went out for a hot second, and came back on. I don't know if y'all know the old wives' tale about the seconds between the flash and the thunder, but supposedly it measures how far the lighting is from you. Less than a second meant it was pretty much on top of us. The lightning had struck our building, and somehow our surge protector to the Micros system failed. The entire POS system was knocked out. Not only were we on handwritten tickets again, but the servers were also having to use the knuckle buster (the old-school credit card slider that imprints your card on a triplicate receipt) to ring everyone up, entailing handwriting their receipts as well. It wasn't a good scene. We couldn't even find our merchant receipts. It had been years since we needed that contraption. We had to go borrow some from next door. Yeah, just put it on the list.

No one was leaving. It's Mobile, what do you do in a torrential downpour?... Stay inside and drink. The bar was standing room only, shots and champagne were flowing. Storm party! Usually these downpours only last ten to fifteen minutes tops. This one went on for over an hour. Downtown is already below sea level, and it was pouring so hard that within minutes the rain flooded the streets, our courtyard and was coming in the building. The dish hole was the worst. It flooded almost immediately. Once it filled up and came into the kitchen, I had to stop food service. I mean we were literally sloshing around in four inches of water with lightning striking all around us. Not a good mix when dealing with electrical equipment.

The day continued in utter craziness. Toni was about to crawl out of her skin. She was used to chaos, but people were now just in her way. That's not a good place for people to be. Now that the kitchen was closed, Marleena was sitting with her favorite customers, sipping on a Budweiser, while Toni was in the back doing Grand Marnier shots to calm her nerves. How do I know this? I was right there with her, of course. We had the bottle. The power flickered on and off, the longest time out being maybe ten minutes. Finally, the rain slacked up and the flood water dispersed as fast as it had come. It was time to shut this circus down.

The worst was after the madness. Our POS system was fried to the point we had to file an insurance claim. It took almost a week to be up and running, keeping the handwritten, knuckle busting system going. We had a stack of receipts that had to be hand-entered into the credit card machine once we were back up. That took Byron about three hours to do. He wasn't a happy camper, bitching the whole time, while I secretly laughed. Poor baby, too much work for him. Oh well.

Reservations?

Ella's parents had made a reservation for twelve people. They specifically requested the bar area and for Toni to wait on them. They had some friends in from out of town and wanted to show off where she worked and the fabulous atmosphere. Even though I was in the kitchen, I always did the seating chart for brunch. This way I assured the reservations kept with the flow and didn't drown the kitchen. I made sure her parents had the tables they wanted and thought all was set.

Midway through brunch, I got to a breaking point and went out to say hello to them and meet their friends. Though I never really considered it, other people did appreciate the owner coming out to talk to them, especially one that worked in the kitchen. I go out to the tables they were supposed to be sitting at, and they weren't there. I found them in the banquet room. Though they didn't complain, they were not happy. They had requested a specific area, with a specific server and I had personally assured them that it was all set. Why were they in the back room? I went to Byron to question this. He just shrugged and basically blew it off. Apparently, he had some friends of his, walk-ins, that wanted the bar area, so he gave their table away and moved them. His response... "They're old, they don't need to be in the bar. It's too loud for them." I was so pissed. I apologized to them, but they knew what happened. It wasn't me.

I was in awe that he was okay with this. This is why we have reservations and a seating chart. That was just blatant disrespect. This is why we had two hostesses, one specifically hired to babysit him. Do not sway from the seating chart. It is strategically set for a reason. The other hostess obviously wasn't doing her job that day. He was going to do whatever he wanted. Why even bother? The next time they came in for brunch, he looked at them and asked, "Do you have reservations?" "Yes, we do Byron, but we came anyway."

Super Bowl

It was Super Bowl Sunday. We decided to have a Super Bowl party after brunch. I know I said I would never do an after-brunch party again, but this was just for our friends. We had the big screen in the dining room, so we moved all the tables around the edge and created a dance floor. Now I couldn't tell you who was playing that year. It was none of our teams. We were having more of a halftime dance party. Madonna was the halftime show, only my favorite performer. I even brought my dog up there, since she was named after my idol. We all brought food and set up for the party.

Just a few of our friends... Right! As everyone got wind of it, knowing our screen across the front of the dining room was the best in town, we got packed. We ended up having to open the bar. We actually sold a shit-ton of drinks, so it was well worth it. The bar next door had the squares, the hottest ticket in town, at $100 a pop. Only one payout at the end... $10,000. Between the two of us, we were rocking the block. So, the halftime show started. All the girls and Madonna (my dog) had a blast dancing in the dining room. Although I was still in kitchen gear, they were all dressed like they were going to a concert, heels and all. Fun time.

The game ended, and one of our regulars won the $10,000! That was awesome. They bought everyone in both bars a shot. We continued this Super Bowl tradition after that. Always a fun time and a nice profit on top of our brunch sales. Why didn't we think of this before?

The Music Festival

We had a huge music festival downtown every year in October. The streets were all blocked off like Mardi Gras. It drew thousands of people, bordering on being way too crowded. We never did much business during this weekend. We had almost decided to close for it, like Fat Tuesday. This went on a little over a decade when suddenly the city pulled the plug and canceled it at the last minute one year. I can't say that as business owners, we were too upset about it. Then out of the blue, a private party decided to invest in their own music festival the same weekend in October. They managed to organize this event in less than a month, complete with some huge headliner acts.

This event was free. Yes, no tickets and even better, no street vendors allowed. They were putting on this festival to help the local businesses. We were the only places that had food and drinks to offer. We knew that we had to do another makeshift fair food situation, items that people could walk around with. This time we could sell it right from our front doors, with no health department issues. The main stage was set up right across the street from us. We were front and center in the event. We didn't know quite what to expect. I mean our courtyard was like front row VIP seating.

The festival lasted Friday through Sunday. Friday night we didn't do too much of our fair food, but we did do a substantial amount of dining room and bar business. Saturday started out slow but gradually picked up throughout the day. We decided not to go crazy with prep for Sunday and just hopefully sell what we had left. So, brunch was coming to an end, and we set up our table at the front doors. Suddenly the floodgates opened. I guess people were leery about a free event, but by Sunday the whole town decided to show up.

The streets were packed. Ava was in front in her angel wings, selling champagne for $5 a cup. We sold out! Polished off almost fifty cases. We couldn't keep our little makeshift bar stocked. Anything we had, we sold. We were in the kitchen throwing together just about anything you could imagine to sell. You talk about clean out the refrigerator. We couldn't keep up! It was crazy. At one point we had sent someone to get pizzas for the staff (you know those $5 pepperoni ones). It was becoming a long day. I go to bring them out and next thing you know, we're selling them for $5 a slice. We rocked it Sunday and couldn't have had a better time. Everybody on the staff split the tips they had made, so they were very happy.

The next year, we knew what to expect. Thanks to the people who believe in supporting the little people, the local businesses, especially the restaurants, we looked forward to this festival for years to come.

The Day the Music Died

Music on Sunday was a must. It helped create the atmosphere. Our Sunday brunch band was not your traditional jazz ensemble. We had Hank and Harold from start to finish. They set up every Sunday in the courtyard and played a jam session. Hank Becker was a celebrity in our parts. He had produced several CDs and was well known in the Mobile music scene. They established the mood and tone of our brunch. Everybody loved them.

Usually dealing with bands is a nightmare for any establishment. I had spent years running a band bar in my pre-restaurant life, and band guys are a breed of their own. Their lifestyle is traditionally stereotyped, with responsibility not being one of their strong points. But not these guys. I hired them in the beginning and never had to deal with the music ever again. They were on autopilot, never missed a beat. On the rare occasion they could not show up, they scheduled their own replacement. We had some awesome musicians over the years—some we would have never been able to afford—thanks to Harold and Hank. They were gold. We were truly blessed to have them.

Although they were scheduled to play from eleven to three, they would often extend that session due to our late-day regular customers. They would tip them, and yes substantially, to turn into a makeshift karaoke session at the end of the day. By that point, it was only the bar and regular customers, and everybody loved it. We would be in the kitchen cleaning and would hear Bon Jovi's "Livin' on a Prayer" and know exactly who was singing. It was one of our favorite couples, and she would murder that song every week. We would almost have paid double to have the band teach her a new song. It was always fun.

In all the years, we only had one Sunday with no music. Hank had been suffering from health problems for years. Sometimes he would show up to play with an oxygen tank in tow, but he never missed a beat. Music was his love, his life. He was an icon in this area. When he passed away, it was a sad day. His funeral was on a Sunday, and we closed the restaurant that morning so everyone could attend. When we all got back, we ended up opening around noon. We put our chalkboard out front and wrote on it: "We will not have live music today, in observance of our dear friend Hank Becker." We played his CDs on a loop that day. His wife was there, as she had always been through the years, and it was a bittersweet but beautiful day. We had all lost a very good friend, a part of the family, but his legacy lived on.

Food Network

We had received several awards throughout our years, but none as surprising and prestigious as when we got voted "Best Breakfast in Alabama" in Food Network Magazine. They did a feature story on fifty states, fifty breakfasts. Apparently, someone had come in and ordered our signature dish, which was our take on an eggs Benedict. It started with a fried grit cake, applewood smoked bacon, poached egg, creole hollandaise sauce and was topped with colossal crab meat sautéed in butter. I will say, it was delicious.

It wasn't like we entered a contest or competition, deciding which breakfast item we would submit. They just notified us that we had won and wanted us to send a picture and description of the dish. It was quite a shock. At first, I didn't even believe it. When we first got the email, I wrote it off, like it was some elaborate sales pitch. Then when they contacted us again, I realized, shit, this is for real. We set up the Benedict and did a little food porn on it. We got an amazing picture and sent it in. When that issue came out, I was on cloud nine. I was ready, this was our first national recognition. I wanted to put a banner across our courtyard, with the Food Network logo on it, "Best Breakfast in Alabama" and under it "Where's Bobby Flay?" Come on, Bobby, bring it. I'm ready. I just knew I could "out-brunch" him. Byron quickly poo-pooed that idea. He was no fun. It was a serious validation of how great our food was, hence the forty-or-so minute wait every Sunday.

Sunday Funday... It was the best!

CH. 4
JUST ANOTHER DAY

SOMETIMES THERE ARE THOSE DAYS that just go too smooth. Don't be fooled. You've heard the phrase "the calm before the storm." That couldn't be truer when it comes to the restaurant world. Just when you think you have smooth sailing, a tidal wave's going to hit and hit hard. It's almost better to have a constant stream of controlled chaos. You get used to that. You live in the moment and wonder what next? On the rare days that seem to be calm, you start to wonder what is wrong? What did we miss? What have we not done? Why is everything working? It'll make you crazy! You need the chaos. Without it, perfection is achieved, and that is just wrong. You can only have perfection in a perfect storm. You have to stay on your toes, and stay alert. Situations are going to happen, and you have to muddle through them the best you can. These are the times that adrenaline kicks in. This is what we live for. This is why we have chosen this as a profession. We are crazy, and that's what it takes. We live to muddle through and get to the end of the night, every night, and finally, belly up to the bar for that coveted libation. In all reality, this is why we drink.

The Hostess

Timing is everything in a restaurant, especially one with a kitchen as big as most people's walk-in closets. The most important aspect of timing starts at the front door: seating. There is a reason we have a hostess. Otherwise, it would just be a free-for-all, guests seating themselves, waiters who may or may not notice them, kitchen getting slammed all at once. You need order to make this flow happen, hence the hostess. It is one of the most important jobs in the restaurant.

Now said hostess is usually some young girl working part-time, not even old enough to serve alcohol. She is the most underpaid person in the restaurant (short of the dishwasher, another key player), usually making minimum wage. Yet this person is entirely, one hundred percent responsible for making or breaking the night. She is in charge of the flow of the restaurant. Screw up the seating, and the restaurant goes down. From the waitstaff being overseated to orders pouring into the kitchen all at once, the seating is key to not having chaos. It's not the most lucrative job, but usually, this person still lives at home with no bills, and it's better than her babysitting gig. Wait, it's really just a different style babysitting.

Now super-ritzy, fine-dining restaurants will generally have a man as their host, a seasoned professional maître d, usually retired from his long career of decades of waiting tables. This man gets it and runs the host stand like a well-oiled machine. He is one of the highest paid people in the restaurant, and for good reason. He is the star of the show, even doing table checks as any good manager would do. But most of us can't afford such luxury, so welcome Barbie girl!

Let's start with the training of the hostess. She must be thoroughly trained in the layout of the restaurant, the table numbers, and server sections. She is instructed to seat a certain number of people (covers) at specified time slots. She is shown how to seat the servers equally and spaces out this seating to give them time to greet each table. Now every restaurant is different. Seating depends on many variables: the menu, number of servers, kitchen size, etc. There is no one magic formula for this process. You have to adapt to what is workable for your size restaurant to keep the flow as smooth as possible. Then the hostess is trained accordingly.

But for all the training, planning, setting, and everything else you can possibly do, there always tends to be a glitch. There really is no such thing as smooth sailing in the restaurant business. On the rare occasion (and these tend to be few and far between) when you have a completely smooth night, where everything flows perfectly, you tend to look around and say, okay, what did we forget? Why was that so easy? There really is no answer. Just take it, pat yourself on the back and say, yeah, we've got this! If the hostess seats the restaurant correctly, that is step one to that magically smooth night. The kitchen will be okay and roll out the food in perfect order as if it were coming off an assembly line. The servers will have perfectly spaced tables and be able to greet and interact with every customer. The environment is completely stress-free. God, we live for these nights.

It all starts with greeting the customers. The hostess is the face at the front door. I don't care what may be going on in your personal life—I know, the complex problems of a seventeen-year-old—always wear a smile. Then the seating process begins. She has to make sure that the servers don't get too swamped. This is why they have sections which allot tables that seat an equal amount of covers. Usually, it's up to the hostess to set these sections each night based on how many servers you have. These sections will be seated in some sort of rotation. A server is only one person. You can't seat three tables in their section at once and expect them to be able to greet each one in a proper amount of time. When a restaurant is in prime-time dinner hours and becomes busy, this flow must continue to happen. So, in comes THE WAIT.

Wait is a four-letter word that might as well start with an "F." The Wait is an integral part of the flow, yet the hostess, and more so the guests, are not always down with it. From the hostess's point of view, she has gone from seating the guests and never having to deal with them again, to moving the guests to a designated area and having to keep up with them until they are seated in their proper place. (Back to babysitting.) So the guests go to the set area, whether it is a bench outside, to the bar to get a cocktail or wherever, and wait. A list is now started so the guests are seated in proper order. God forbid couple "B" is seated before couple "A." "A" was there ten minutes before they were, and believe me, they know. The guests typically do not like The Wait, which could easily be avoided if they had just bothered to make a reservation. Once The Wait has commenced, it all flows back to the hostess and her charming ability to keep everybody happy. A good hostess can rock The Wait in her sleep. This is where they shine. Their adrenaline rush kicks in and the challenge of moving and shaking everything to perfection begins. A good hostess loves The Wait. It takes an otherwise dull night and turns it into a game, a game they can master and win, patting themselves on the back at the end of the night because they played it so well.

The guests don't see it that way at all. Many times, The Wait kicks in when there are clearly empty tables in the restaurant. They cannot understand why they just can't sit at one of those empty tables. Well people, let me explain the many reasons these tables are not being seated the minute you walk in the door.

1. Each server just got sat in the last two minutes and needs time to greet these tables before another one is sat in their section. Do you really want to be escorted to a table, only to sit for five to ten minutes before a server acknowledges you? No, you will become annoyed. So, go to the bar, get a drink, and in those minutes, you now have had human interaction (the bartender), service (drinks in hand), and when the hostess comes to seat you, you are already happy.

2. These tables are reserved for guests that actually planned ahead. They called to make reservations (I know, a rare occurrence, especially in the South) ensuring that a table would be ready for them at their chosen time, hence avoiding The Wait. We can't very well seat you at that table when it is reserved in fifteen minutes.

3. The kitchen has gone down in flames (not literally, most of the time) for whatever reason, and cannot handle any more tickets at this time. Again, if you are seated, your server promptly greets you, you get your drinks, but your food takes an hour, you are annoyed.

4. Some server has called in sick at the last minute, leaving the restaurant short-staffed. That section is probably closed. Or someone in the kitchen has called in. (Hell, it's the kitchen. They don't even pretend to be sick. You're lucky if they called in at all.) This leaves the kitchen man down and everyone scrambling to do two jobs at once. Again, do you really want to wait an hour on your food? They just need a smidgen of time to catch up.

For whatever the reason, The Wait has gone into effect, and there is nothing you can do about it. A good hostess can do this, and work it like a rockstar. In a perfect world, another great, smooth-as-possible night. 'Nuff said! Unfortunately, these hostesses are a rarity. They are like some mythical creature you've heard about but haven't ever seen, like the Snuffleupagus on Sesame Street. Who really ever saw him? Big Bird, so he did exist! So do great hostesses. When you find one, grab her, keep her, take care of her, make it worth her while. It will save you beaucoups in the long run. It is one of the most important jobs in the restaurant... FOR REAL!

Let me give you an example of a typical night, with your typical hostess. Did I mention Barbie girl? She's too young and too cute to care what's going on. She spends most of her time on her phone because God forbid you are out of touch with social media for a five-hour shift. The whole world could have changed, and you missed it over this stupid job that your mom made you take to teach you some sort of responsibility. And Mom is friends with the owner, so you have to act like you care. She just wants to seat these people and get them out of her hair. Now they are someone else's problem.

Here we go. Table for four? Okay, right this way. Oh, did I forget to tell a server that I just sat these people in a closed section? Oh my God, look. I just sat the whole restaurant, all at once. So proud! Now, these people can wait, I'm on autopilot. This job is cake. Wait, did I just chip a nail? Crisis! Have to go to the bathroom and touch it up, I can't seat any more people right now anyway.

"Where is the hostess?" People mill around with no direction as to what to do. Okay, she's finally back. What? You had a reservation? Oops, I've already sat that table. It didn't even occur to me to look at that book. Who makes reservations on a Tuesday night anyway? You'll have to wait. Sorry.

Being a kitchen person, I especially like it when the ticket machine starts printing and NEVER stops... NOT! Here's what is going down behind those doors, thanks to our lovely hostess. Suddenly tickets are pouring in, dragging the floor, and they keep going like the Energizer bunny! We are officially drowning! Are you kidding me? Who is seating this restaurant? Go get the hostess! What do you mean you can't find her? Oh, chipped a nail?... Didn't realize we had a bona fide emergency on our hands! My bad. Hope you have all informed your tables that it will be a hot minute before they get their food.

Let's prioritize.

"Any tables NOT drinking?" For God's sake, mark their tickets. Let's bump them to the top of the line. There is no way to keep them entertained

RESTAURANT... FOR REAL

and happy. "Can we buy you a shot of water?"

"Okay, any pregnant people?" They definitely go to the front of the line. They're eating for two.

"Wait, there's an event tonight? Starts at seven? Can we please figure out who is going to this event and mark their tickets?" Let's at least try to get them out of here on time. Oh, and if any of these event-goers actually made a reservation (and got seated), they definitely get top of the line priority.

"Has anyone seen the hostess yet?"

Okay, muddling along, finally pulled the tickets off the floor. Hope we didn't lose any.

"Yes, I know table 12 is complaining, so are tables 15, 8, 24, 3, and 9! Get in fucking line!"

"Buy table three a round of drinks. What do you mean they aren't drinking? Why is their ticket not marked?"

"Here send them this app we were about to sell to table 8 and buy them a round. I know the show starts in twenty minutes. I can't shit a well-done ribeye!"

"Really? You forgot to ring in table 21? In the middle of this? Are you kidding? And let me guess, another well-done ribeye... Seriously?" I was kidding. Clearly you aren't. "Shit! Sure, we can get that on the fly" NOT! (Remind me to fire the hostess.) I don't care that she's my best friend's daughter.

"Where are all these people coming from? Do we even seat this many people? Where are they sitting? On the roof?"

"I know, I know, the show. Cancel table 12? Just comp their drinks and apologize. Someone run this food! Food is dying!" (Someone slit my wrists.)

"Okay, here's your well-fucking-done ribeye on they fly. What do you mean they are leaving? I personally threw this shit in the fryer to cook it faster! Oh, I almost forgot. It took you twenty-five minutes to put their order in."

"Table 4 is complaining their food is cold? Would that be the food that sat in the window for fifteen minutes? Of course, it's cold!" (Fuck firing her, slit the hostess's wrists.)

"We need plates!"

"NO! Don't start seating The Wait, they aren't getting any food any time soon anyway. Let them drink!"

"Special order, my ass! Yeah, they are the ONLY table in this restaurant"... I have all the time in the world to create their custom menu for them."

"I seriously don't have time for this vegan bullshit right now!"

"Who the fuck brought a baby out this late? Of course, he's screaming. Bring that kid something to shut him up!"

Slowly trying to crawl up to the top of the water. We can almost see it now, just can't quite get there yet. Need to breathe. Keep going! Another special order? This night is so fucked! Oh, the hostess has once again graced us with her presence? Nail okay? All your friends okay? Can you maybe finish doing your job? Get us through this godawful night!

Finally, broke through! We're treading water now. We can breathe. About to crawl out and dry off. This nightmare is almost over. Shots for the kitchen!... Did I mention, this is why we drink!

In summary of this night, we comped six tables' drinks, three tables' appetizers, two entire tables' food and drinks and had three walkouts! This lovely hostess cost us about $500 that one night. But her nail survived! Like I said, when you find a good one...

It would have been an altogether different, and somewhat pleasant evening had the hostess followed The Wait. People, we in the restaurant world are not here to test your patience. We are not making bets in the back to see how long we can make you wait. We are not maliciously picking you out of the crowd because we don't like your outfit. We genuinely care to get you out in time to catch that show.

The Wait is a good thing, a positive thing. It should be embraced. We are trying to make your dining experience the best it can possibly be. We want you to be attended to and taken care of. We do care about these things. Short of sounding like a Delta airline steward... "You have a choice in where you dine, and where you choose to spend your hard-earned money. Thank you for flying (I mean dining) with us. We hope you have had a lovely experience." Embrace The Wait. That means we care. We don't want you to have to use your seat cushion as a flotation device because we're drowning.

Guest Dishwasher

Downtown was a unique environment. All the other bar and restaurant owners stuck together and helped each other out. It was like our own secret society, the original "rat pack" who built it and paved the way for it to be okay and safe for people to venture down there. One of the original members was a good friend of mine, Danny. He had opened a sports bar about a year before we opened the restaurant. I actually helped him get it started. I set up his books, inventories, payroll... the whole nine yards. It was a struggle back then. He didn't handle the stress too well at all. He was a little high strung, and most of his employees were scared of him. He would rant and rave at any given moment about sometimes the most minute things, like a pepper shaker not all the way full. I swore he was going to explode one day when his blood pressure climbed sky high from all the stress.

One day in the midst of one of these rants, he ventured down to my restaurant. My dishwasher was a no-show that day, so we were all rotating like crazy running the machine to keep up. He put on an apron and started washing dishes. It seemed to calm him. Suddenly he was in a Zen state of doing a mindless task, rinse, wash, sanitize, dry, and put up. He stayed the whole shift. Called his place and told them not to disturb him, he was busy. I'm sure they didn't mind. (Keep him there). He decided that he needed to have that shift on a weekly basis. He told me he would come to do dishes for me every Friday, and his pay would be three Red Stripes. I know, he was soooooo expensive, but good help is hard to find, right?

So, he settled into his new shift, and took it very seriously. His staff loved the fact they could count on a break while he was there, and they knew not to disturb him. Short of his building burning down, they wouldn't dare. I really never thought it would last, but he showed up like clockwork. For months he was our guest dishwasher, for three Red Stripes a shift. I guess for him it was a break from the constant pressure of owning your own business, just doing something mindless and checking out for a while. Hell, I don't blame him, I have worked that dish hole many nights, and it is almost like therapy, no thinking... just doing.

Finally, the day came when he had to give me his notice. He actually worked out his last two weeks, then back to his place to deal with the constant headaches of restaurant ownership. I think he missed that little break. I know I missed him. Good luck finding another dishwasher that would work for that kind of "pay."

Just One Finger

Kitchens are dangerous places. We work in an environment where there are fire, grease, and sharp objects. It's inevitable that eventually, accidents will happen. One evening we were slammed and not prepped for it. I got out the mandolin to slice an order of sweet potato chips on the fly. Now we all know that this is an evil instrument, especially the commercial models which don't come with a guard. Caution should be taken. There should at minimum be a wet rag under the foot to keep it from slipping. You should also take the precaution to wear a metal glove to prevent cutting your finger off. Should, being the key word here.

Now I half-ass look around for a rag to use, but I only have my dry one. Dry towels are a commodity in the kitchen. They are your hot pads. Once it gets even the slightest bit damp, you will burn the shit out of yourself trying to grab something out of a 400-degree convection oven. So, I give up looking and am not going to sacrifice my dry towel. I set up the mandolin and decide that I could anchor it with my boobs. I know, not the best plan but I really was too busy to rethink that one. I go to slicing these chips and sure enough... It slips. I was in the downward motion of the slice, and although it seemed like an eternity, it was a split-second. I knew in my head what was about to happen and there wasn't a damn thing I could do about it. Next thing you know it sliced right through my pinky finger. It was such a clean, sharp slice that it took about five seconds to actually start bleeding. I grabbed my finger and held it up as blood started pouring down my arm. I had to get out of the kitchen.

One of our regulars was there and thank God she was a nurse. She took me to the back room to assess the situation. I finally let go and let her look at it. The whole side of my finger was sliced off to the bone, with only a thin piece of skin hanging on. I turned white as a ghost. It was the only time in my life I can recall feeling like I was going to faint. Blood was going everywhere. She immediately made a call and rushed me to the emergency room where she had a friend of hers waiting. He was a plastic surgeon. He literally stitched my finger back on. Twenty-eight stitches! He told me that I'd probably never have any feeling left in it, but at least it wouldn't look deformed. Thank God for her. Any random ER visit would have resulted in them just snipping the whole thing off, and I would have had a bone finger.

When it was time to remove the stitches, we were outside in the court-yard of the restaurant. She took them out as the entire happy hour crowd watched. It was that day's amusement. Everyone was in awe that it looked so good. It looked good, but the doctor was right. I have absolutely no feeling in that finger. To this day, I have never touched a mandolin again. I would rather eat worms. Evil contraption!

Sweet as Honey

Burns are an equally common hazard in the kitchen. There are just so many ways you can burn yourself. The worst is hot grease. I was on sauté/fry one night, and we were running our soft-shell crab special. That was an item that came and went from the menu based on the price and availability. We had these beautiful jumbo-sized crabs, about five inches wide. I used to hate frying them. We'd dust them in our seasoned flour and gently lower them into the fryer to assure they were spread out to the fullest capacity. Most of the time they were fine, but every so often water would get caught under the shell. You know the saying, "Water and oil don't mix." Just a simple drop of water in that hot grease makes it spit at you like crazy. So, I lowered the crab in, and it spit. I'm talking a millimeter from my eye and splattered down my cheek. (So lucky on that one) It was a bad one.

I had just met this older woman chef who had told me a story about the worst burn she had ever gotten in a kitchen, where the grease splattered all over her face. Now I'm looking at this woman wondering how much plastic surgery she had had because her skin was flawless, simply beautiful. And no, she wasn't wearing makeup. She told me the secret, and it's the best advice I think I've ever been given, based on my profession. Honey, pure raw honey. She immediately rubbed honey on her face and it never even blistered. No scarring. Nothing. Like it never happened. Boy, would I have liked to have known that trick before now. Before all the burn scars most chefs have from their elbow to their hands, and for me down my leg.

I thought of this story and immediately grabbed the honey and slathered it down my face. We kept the typical burn cream in the first aid kit, but that close to my eye I wasn't feeling it. Too many chemicals and God knows what else. The rest of the night, in that hot-ass corner, I could feel the sticky running down my face and occasionally in my eye. It wasn't pleasant, but it worked. I put a towel on my pillow that night and went to sleep with a fresh slathering of honey. The next morning, I woke up and there was no blistering, no bubbles. It was red but smooth. After a couple of days of this, it was gone, like it never happened. Honey. I strongly recommend keeping that behind your line. It works!

Health Inspector

It was Friday lunch. Monty had come in, still up from the night before, still fucked up from the night before. He was doing no one any good, so I sent him to the back room to sleep it off. We started to get slammed. Duane noticed that the cooler wasn't holding temp. We were trying to get to a breaking point so we could throw the food in an ice chest until we could figure out what was up. There were about fifteen tickets hanging and I looked up… in walked the health inspector. She always had the knack of the worst possible timing. Now when the health inspector comes in, they expect 100% of your attention. It doesn't matter what you are doing, you drop everything and focus solely on them. Okay, here we go.

She started off in the kitchen and sure enough, checked the temps of the items in the cooler. Of course, they are too high. She decided that we have to throw everything in the cooler away. She made us get the nastiest trash can from outside and watched us as we pull everything and throw it in. Usually, there were just a few items in that cooler, enough to get us through a shift. This particular day we had a rehearsal dinner later that night so planning ahead, I had brought over eight filets, intending to butcher them after lunch to prep for it. Well, now they were garbage. We had to tell Katie that lunch service was pretty much over at this point. I had Duane call to get the cooler repaired.

Now she was walking around with me. First, to the bar. Thank God everything was in check there. Next to the bathrooms and dining room. Finally, back to the banquet room. And there was Monty, passed out on a row of chairs looking like something the cat wouldn't have even brought in. She wasn't amused as this wasn't her first rodeo with my fucked-up employees. At least he wasn't puking. This was not looking good for us. She was making notes on her little clipboard then proceeded to walk into the stock room. Now, this is when the restaurant next door was being built. The construction had stirred up the mice which had apparently been living contentedly there until now. We were in the process of having the whole block exterminated. As I'm standing there talking to her, a mouse runs across the room behind her. We are so done. She wants to talk and talk, and all I can think is get her out of this room. Thank God she didn't notice the mouse.

We went back to the kitchen so she could write up her report. Needless to say, it wasn't the highest score, but not low enough to shut us down. After a severe reprimanding about cooler temps and employee conduct, she finally left. Now it was crunch time. I had to go to the local meat market to replace the filets we had to throw away and yes, pay retail for them. There goes the profit on this party. By the time I returned, Monty had graced us with his hungover presence, trying to half-ass re-prep the cooler items. The cooler was back up to temp. The problem? It had somehow come unplugged. Seriously, the repairman got there and plugged it in, to the tune of $125 service call. These are the days that make me wonder... Why do I love this?

Just One Day Off

So, I had planned with Sarah a grand birthday party for her husband. We had made reservations at the chef's table at the hot new fine-dining restaurant on top of the largest hotel downtown. This place was all glass-enclosed, offering beautiful views of the city. We were so excited. We made these reservations three months in advance, right when they opened. I had scheduled myself off on a Saturday night for God's sake. That never happened. The chef's table was in high demand, the first in Mobile. It only sat six people, so Sarah chose her guest list wisely, me because not only were she and I close friends, but as a chef, I would appreciate sitting in the kitchen watching all the action going on around me. I brought a date of my choosing, which Sarah was leery about my choices, and her husband's two best friends. We won't even discuss my date. It was a catastrophe, as usual. My downfall has always been my taste in men, but I never had time to seriously date anyway.

We were so excited to sit at this coveted table and celebrate his birthday. I raided Val's closet and sported the blue Manolos. I actually did my hair (okay, I had it done) and put on makeup. I had on a fabulous designer cocktail dress and was ready to make our grand appearance, representing my restaurant to the nines. The only mistake we made, which all of us thought was a good idea at the time, was going to my restaurant first to have a pre-dinner cocktail. We got there, and all hell started breaking loose. Leah was hosting in her "go out on a Saturday night outfit," which tells me already that someone didn't show up. Turns out we were one server and one kitchen person down. They were struggling.

Of course, I could not just sit there and do nothing, so I pulled up my hair, got in the kitchen and helped expo the line. Not my first rodeo in a cocktail dress and heels. I helped prep the food, plate the food, and ran the food. I was sweating my ass off, forget hair and makeup. I helped Amber get out of the weeds from twenty something martinis coming in all at once. It was crazy. I was so close to telling Sarah that I couldn't make it, or at least I'd see them there later. She just gave me a look. She knew if they left me there, they would never see me again. Get in the car Chelle, you're not even supposed to be here, we've been planning this for three months! She was right, they were going down, and I at least helped to get them to almost treading water, but really, not much else I could do. And Byron sure as hell wasn't coming in. They'd already called him. So I left and hoped for the best.

It was hard. The first twenty minutes or so that we were at the new restaurant, I was stressed. Then the food started coming out in courses, and the chef came out to explain his vision. It was fabulous. I almost forgot what a shit-show I'd left behind. We wined and dined. Of course, they knew who I was, one of my previous sous-chefs was working there. So, I got the grand tour of all the behind-the-scenes workings. The second time that night I'm in Manolos in the kitchen. That place was huge, they had twenty people on the line. It made me proud to think of what we did in our little walk-in closet with three to five people. And the food was fabulous. It far exceeded our expectations. We settled the bill (by the way, my date forgot his credit card... go figure), tipped the chef, and went back to the restaurant for a nightcap. Okay my idea, I just wanted to make sure that they had survived the chaos. The crew looked like they had been run over by a freight train. But they had survived. I bought them all a round of drinks and thanked them. I had such a great team, and I was thankful for that.

ABC

The ABC, Alabama Beverage Control Board, were always a pain in the ass. They were the perfect example of giving a man a badge and a gun. I swear the only requirement for that job was to have a two-inch dick. Any bigger and they wouldn't have been so angry. They loved to fuck with everybody, quoting laws that had been on the books for two hundred years. I mean seriously, in Mobile there was still a law that states women cannot wear heels downtown.

All the bars and restaurants had a call system, warning everybody when they showed up. (We also had this system for the health department inspectors. We were a team downtown, and had to look out for each other)

One Friday night, in the middle of Art Walk, they showed up. Art Walk is an event the second Friday every month that showcased local artists, who set up in front of businesses and galleries. It was always crowded with people downtown checking out the scene. Very family friendly. We had a rehearsal dinner that night for about seventy-five people. The restaurant was packed, and here they came.

They stormed in the doors. Literally, kicked the doors open. There were four of them, and they were decked out in riot gear. Seriously, bulletproof vests, helmets, boots, all in black with their guns, clubs, and flashlights. They immediately go behind the bar. They pushed Amber away and start slamming open the beer cooler doors, shining their flashlights in them. They stormed through the dining room to the back room where we had our formal banquet going on. Next thing I know I'm summoned out of the kitchen to be informed that they are writing me a citation because I had two bottles of the same wine open. Of course, I had two bottles. Shit, I probably had six or seven. It was a banquet with a beer and wine package, and there were seventy-five people. Are they serious? Another ancient, irrelevant law.

The customers were in utter shock at this spectacle. They had their families eating here. It looked like the ABC had gotten some hot tip that we were cooking crystal meth in the kitchen, the way they were acting. Two bottles of wine? Are you serious? Okay, go ahead and take me to prison. Clearly I'm a danger to society. The rehearsal dinner guests were mortified! But I tell you, they will definitely have a story to tell once the initial shock wears off. (And if the marriage doesn't last, they can blame it on bad karma that night.)

I've never seen anything like it. Riot gear at a fine-dining restaurant. I guarantee they never stormed into other establishments outside of the downtown area like that—a fact I brought up when I had to meet with them to dispute the ridiculous citation. Apparently one of our customers that night was appalled enough to make a phone call. He was there with his children for God's sake. He was an influential man. We not only got out of the citation, they never bothered us again. When they did ever come into the restaurant after that, they wore nice polo shirts and khaki pants. It was about time they learned a little respect.

Curfew

It was in the middle of the power outage of hurricane Ivan. The waters were still pretty high. Most everyone was holed up at my house. Katie and I were going to check on the restaurant. Now her car was down, and I drive a convertible. We were getting nowhere in my car, so we borrowed my roommate's truck. It was an old-school Nissan, with the bench seat. The only problem was the seat was set to his six-foot ass and wouldn't move. We get in the truck and head downtown. It was only three miles from my house so it wouldn't be that bad. I'm driving the truck practically laying down on the seat, pushing the pedals with my toe. I can barely see through the windshield. We make it downtown, and all is good with the restaurant.

We decided to go down to the one bar that was open and running on a generator. At least we could charge our phones and have a drink. There was a mandatory curfew at the time, but the business owners had already decided that it didn't apply to us. I mean it was set to help curtail looting in all these closed businesses, and we had every right to protect our own places. It was past curfew and we were heading back to my house. It was dark, and I was having a really hard time seeing because of the way I had to drive the truck. Katie decided I needed to scootch up to the edge of the seat and she sat behind me, legs straddling me, so I could lean against her. We were laughing so hard at the scenario of getting pulled over. She would lean over to search the glove box, ass in the air... she had a great ass. I would lean on the window, showing cleavage for days and talk to the officer. Tits and ass, how could we have a problem?

Well, as we were cracking ourselves up as to how that would play out, we heard the siren. Oh yeah, we were getting pulled over. Time to put this plan into effect. What the hell. Katie leaned over and started digging through the glove box for the registration, and I adjusted my top for the ultimate cleavage. When the cop came up to the window, we realized it was Dean. He had worked at the restaurant waiting tables while he was going through the police academy. He was family. He just laughed when he realized it was us. Okay girls, what the hell are you doing? You know it's past curfew. Yeah, we know, whatever. He pretended to scold us, then laughed at our tits and ass routine and told us to go home.

Okay, off we go. But we had one more stop to make at a friend's house. We had some looting to do of our own. We needed vodka. Vodka is a key hurricane supply. Probably the most important. And we were out at my house. Our friend was out of town, and we knew where she hid the key, so we looted the vodka and some Jager too. We left her a note: "You've been looted. Took the Grey Goose and the Jager. Love you, Chelle & Katie." I mean if friends can't loot from friends? And back to the house we went. Just another day in the aftermath of a hurricane.

Valentine's Day Fire

It was a Saturday, in the middle of Mardi Gras and it was Valentine's Day. Even though parades were going on all around us, we had a packed brunch. The weather was perfect, and the courtyard was the hottest ticket in town for your Valentine's date. The Bloody Mary bar was going, the champangel was flitting, live music was playing. It couldn't have been a more perfect day... Should have knocked on wood at that very moment.

We were winding down brunch. It was after three o'clock, and the grill was still full of steaks and burgers. We were trying to finish cooking these last orders so we could shut down and regroup the kitchen for dinner service that night. We were booked solid, and our first reservations started in less than two hours at five o'clock.

As on any busy Saturday, the grill started to flame up. Sam did the usual. She squirted it with water, but it flamed right back up. She grabbed the salt... not working, then the baking soda... not working. Nothing was working. She was trying to maneuver the food around the flames so as not to completely char them. She turned off the grill because the fire was getting out of control. She started frantically trying to pull the food off the grill amidst the flames. I grabbed two more boxes of baking soda and start dumping them on the fire.

The flames were getting bigger and higher. They were spreading across the entire grill. Suddenly we realize we may have a problem, Houston. No more getting out of control. It was out of control. We were about to have a full-on fire on our hands. Paco grabbed the fire extinguisher. He backed up all the girls behind him. As he was pulling the clip on the extinguisher, a huge flame flared up. It looked like a tidal wave of fire. It caught the salamander broiler above the grill, and all hell broke loose. The kitchen is officially on fire!

For a split-second, we thought we were about to blow up. But not so much. The trusty ANSUL system went into full gear. I can't say that I've ever seen this system in full force. I've always worked around them, had them serviced each year, but never put much thought into how (or if) they actually worked. Oh, they work!

So as the tidal wave of fire encompasses the entire grill/salamander set-up, the system goes off. Suddenly the entire kitchen is getting sprayed with this white foamy powder. It looked like it was snowing. It definitely put out the fire and totally killed our kitchen. Everything was covered in this white shit, including all the food we were cooking. The only thing salvageable was Ella's pizzas and French toast in the oven. We were all standing there in complete shock. What the fuck just happened?

We are fucked! There was no plan B, C, or D for this. If the ice machine goes out, go grab some bags from the gas station. If the cooler goes down, no problem. Grab the ice chests and keep rolling. If the fryer goes out, we change up the menu a bit and break out the cast iron skillets. Someone no-shows, we call in someone else. These are typical situations that every restaurant owner has had to deal with. You can't stress. It's just part of the business. We are used to these issues and typically have a plan. I mean shit happens. But the kitchen just caught on fire? What now? Where's that plan, besides call it a day and be done? And to top it off, the customers are asking about their food. Well people, you're not getting your food. It's covered in some sort of white chemicals.

Looking back on this day, I think this whole situation could have been avoided had we stopped seating people at three when brunch was officially over. We could have shut down and cleaned the grill which had been overloaded all day to begin with. We wouldn't have had those extra forty items on the grill after three. But I was nice. It was Valentine's Day. That was the straw.

It was three thirty at this point. Late brunch people are not happy. We pulled the food out of the oven and did what we could. We now have about an hour and a half to get this place ready for dinner service. So we go to work, all hands on deck, front and back of the house. We pull the grill apart, drain and clean the fryer, wipe down everything. Then we basically hosed out the kitchen. Took almost an hour but with the whole crew there, we did it. The kitchen was spotless as if nothing had ever happened. We were forty minutes out from the first reservations. We had already butchered the filets, ribeyes, and fish. Most of everything was prepped. Okay, let's do this, Valentine's round two. We're ready!

We go to turn on all the equipment and nothing! Apparently when the ANSUL system goes off, it automatically shuts off your gas lines. Good to know this safety feature exists. Good to know we wouldn't have blown up. Also, would have LOVED to have known that we had no working kitchen equipment, and not a snowball's chance in hell of being able to open back up before we spent an hour cleaning it!

Side note: Only the gas company can turn your lines back on. And only after the ANSUL system has been inspected, reloaded, and cleared by the fire department. NOT happening on a Saturday night, in the middle of Mardi Gras. Couldn't get that done until Monday. By the way, Sunday morning we had a little help from a friend who got our gas lines up and running for brunch then disconnected it again for the gas company to "inspect." Wish we had thought of our friend that night.

At this point we begin to panic. We have been booked solid for weeks. It's Valentine's night, one of the single busiest nights of the year, especially for our style of restaurant. We have no equipment to cook on! Kameron comes in the kitchen cradling the reservation book to his chest like it's a newborn baby. He's rocking back and forth muttering, "Soooooooo, should I start calling people?" Really, it's now about thirty minutes until service, we are about to RUIN these people's Valentine's night, and they damn sure aren't going to get a reservation anywhere else decent anyway. Oh my God, this a nightmare! I'm desperately trying to remain calm. No problems. No problems. No problems. I kept telling myself that, but I was starting not to believe it anymore.

What the hell are we going to do now? Then suddenly the plan unfolds. I'm sure that we can only call this "Plan Pull-it-out-of-your-ass!" because there is no B, C, D, or even Z that can even begin to come close to this one. A grill! We need a good old grill! Who hasn't grilled steaks in the backyard? Thank God Toni and Kameron lived right around the corner. They went to the house to get theirs, no driving involved, they just rolled it down the street. The grill had one sauté burner on the side, perfect.

Let's recap. It's Saturday night, Valentine's Day, and Mardi Gras. Parades are going on all around us. Roads are closed, people are tailgating, and our parking lot was packed! Lucky for us, a friend of mine had come down a few days earlier and claimed two parking spaces by our back door to park his camper. Well, part of that space was now mine. We set up the grill right outside the door in the parking lot and cranked it up. We pulled a cooler out there with all the food, and we were in business. We were NOT going to ruin these people's Valentine's Day! I had to completely do a set menu that worked with our new makeshift "kitchen," and I must say it turned out fabulous!

The grill was hot, the menu was set, we are starting to seat the guests. Here we go. The health department was out in full force every Mardi Gras parade night, checking the vendors' carts and food trucks. I had to look like a tailgater. No, I'm not cooking two hundred steaks for this restaurant behind me, I just have a lot of friends. Katie found a t-shirt for me to wear so I could get out of my uniform. I put on a bunch of Mardi Gras beads (you have to look like part of the tailgater crowd) and commenced to cooking. I'm flipping Pontchartrains (a fabulous seafood dish) about four at a time on the one burner I had to work with and grilling steaks to perfection. I'm passing the steaks from the parking lot through the dish hole screaming the cook temps so guys on the line in the kitchen could plate them up. Luckily our oven was electric, so we were able to heat up mashed potatoes, asparagus, and sauces to keep them warm in hot boxes in the kitchen.

The guys from the restaurant next door kept coming out to smoke and giving me hell. I lit a cigarette and kept grilling. I mean I was already breaking every health code you could imagine, why not smoke… I was a little stressed out. I couldn't believe that we pulled this off, but we did. We didn't miss a beat. Not one send back. It was an interesting night, to say the least. Over the next few weeks, I kept running into customers that told me they ate there Valentine's night and it was the best meal they have ever had. Really? Okay, I'll take it. No one on the other side of those doors even knew the hell we went through to ensure they had a wonderful evening. They had a great dining experience. Like I've said, sometimes that perfect plate is a lot more work than you realize.

We cleaned up and toasted to an awesome night. What's a little kitchen fire? Plan Pull-it-out-of-your-ass was a complete success! Forget the fact that half my staff needed a Xanax to get through the night… Just kidding… Just another day.

CH. 5
GET THIS PARTY STARTED

WHENEVER YOU ARE PLANNING ANY KIND OF PARTY or event, you start with the food and bar. Once you eliminate the more formal, seated dinner you have the buffet option. It seems simple enough. You pick some food and let the guests serve themselves. I've never been a big fan of the buffet personally. As a restaurant person, yes, it's easy enough, even fun, to get out and set up. You get to create all the different risers, decorate these amazing looking platters and have them laid out to a T, absolutely beautiful. Better take some pictures, because it ain't gonna last.

Any venue that offers this option has strategically planned and printed menus, specifying quantities, whether it be per piece (hors d'oeuvres) or per person (large quantity items in a chafing dish). The first step is to determine what time of day the event will take place. If it's an afternoon shower around three-ish, light hors d'oeuvres are completely acceptable, since you are in that magic zone between lunch and dinner.

Now I don't care what people's eating habits are, when it comes to anything free, suddenly they eat three square meals a day, breakfast, lunch, and dinner. If your event takes place within these hours, don't think you can skimp on some light hors d'oeuvres. People expect food, and lots of it! We once had a banquet manager who would let the guests order whatever they wanted. Big mistake! People need to be told how much food they need for a certain number of guests. Left to their own devices, they will run out of food before half the guests have made their way through the line. That is just a simple fact of human nature. When something is free, people load up on it—not necessarily eat it but load up on it. It's a shame how much food is thrown out at a buffet party. I don't care if someone is flat-out allergic to shrimp, they put at least four of them on their plate, just to be thrown away by the servers.

So now that we've established how much we are going to have to feed these people, you choose the menu and type of service. The best parties have a balance between hors d'oeuvres and chafing dishes. Say for an average party of forty people, order a good, hearty entrée, like a jambalaya, lasagna, or carved meat station and build around that. Offer a salad, and definitely, some substantial sides like mac and cheese, vegetable gratin or a mashed potato bar, especially if you're doing carved meats. Always have a few hors d'oeuvres at the beginning of the table like a cheese plate, a dip, pinwheels, skewers, stuffed mushrooms... the list goes on and on. Last, throw in a dessert tray, and you have the perfect party food.

I can't stress how important it is to pick the right quantities. There is a reason these menus are priced per person. We did not just spin a wheel and come up with some random prices. This is not our first rodeo. We've done this a few times and know what people eat. Isn't that why you host your event at an established venue to begin with? Not just have some throw down shindig in your backyard? Trust that we know what you need. Event planning is our specialty, not yours. There is nothing worse than running out of food halfway through your party.

Here is how your typical buffet party plays out. There is a mingling period where everyone gets a cocktail and stands around greeting people. This cocktail time usually lasts about thirty to forty-five minutes. Then somehow, like magic, the buffet line begins. No one makes an announcement, rings a bell or anything. It's like a mental clock just goes off in your head... Ding... Food time.

As soon as the buffet line opens, the guests start loading those little plates with as much food as they possibly can. Again, human nature. They aren't going to eat it, mind you, but they damn sure are going to have it. It's free. Buffets bring out the worst in human nature—wasteful and selfish. Round one at the buffet should have ample food for all your guests to eat and to throw away. Yes, a third of the food you bought just goes to the garbage.

Again, if not enough food is ordered, halfway through the line the guests are left with scraps, leaving them starving. These guests won't stay too long. They are ready to go get something to eat. So when you are cutting the cake at nine o'clock wondering where half your guests went, the answer is simple… to eat! Had you ordered enough food, they would still be there singing "Happy whatever" to their heart's content. And the guests don't realize that it's their cheap host who fucked this up, so they blame the restaurant. It's not good for business to have the reputation that if we host your party, you'll starve to death. This is where a good banquet manager shines. I've had some poor ones, but when Kameron came on board, he was the best. He never let people dictate to him. He took control of the situation and made sure they ordered the proper quantities. People listened to him. They loved him.

Once that line has begun, the constant battle of keeping it clean begins. People kill me the way they lay all kinds of dirty glasses, plates, and used napkins right there on the food table. It's so disgusting. Servers spend half their time bussing the food tables in an almost failed attempt to keep it clean and tidy. In general, people just don't care. You have to wonder what they do at home? Who takes a bite out of something then sits it back down by the platter of food? And when there are children involved, that's a whole different situation. If there are going to be a few kids, the best plan is a separate table, away from the adults, for their chicken fingers and fries. Otherwise, let's go back to human nature. Parents tend to let the kids run rampant in the buffet line, touching everything with their dirty, little, nose picking hands. They destroy the table with little or no regard for any kind of manners. Hands down, the buffet brings out the worst in people.

Weddings

Banquets are a whole different animal in the restaurant world. First of all, there is always some sort of occasion: birthday, anniversary, sweet 16, engagement, retirement, promotion, going away, various showers… the list goes on and on. Some banquets are more elaborate than others, but one thing is common—this is the end-all, be-all event of their life. Perfection must happen, or the event is ruined. Oh, and they are the first people to ever host such an event. Do we clearly understand what they are doing? After thousands of banquets I daresay I've pretty much seen it all. But the wedding definitely tops the list as the most complicated of any event.

From the get-go, this is a situation you size up carefully. At the first meeting, you usually meet with at least the bride. Now some of these wives-to-be will come with entourage in tow: mom, grandmother, sister, cousin, future mother-in-law, best friend (usually the maid of honor), any close gay man in her life, etc. Upon initial meeting, you must first size up the party and decide one thing and one thing only: who's in charge, or rather, who's on first? You know that slapstick comedy routine? Yeah, it's really like that sometimes.

Don't be fooled that just because the bride is the one giving up her independence to become "Mrs. Tom Smith," just because she should be the VIP of the wedding, her show, her day, shit—her wedding, that doesn't mean squat when there is the entourage. You never stupidly assume that she is going to make all (or any) of the decisions. Especially when her future mother-in-law is involved.

Now some brides are fortunate enough to have made some sort of con- nection with said in-law. They have bonded, become best friends. Their baby boy is marrying someone they just love and adore. Someone who will continue to take care of him as if he never left home. These relationships are so rare, like the unicorn.

Don't be fooled. One wrong choice and the bride becomes the mortal enemy. The future mother-in-law almost always means the kiss of death. I've always felt bad for those brides who actually think that involving them will somehow strengthen their relationship. Traditionally, the groom's family pays for the rehearsal dinner, and the bride's family pays for the wedding. When you cross these worlds, it's almost always a bad ending for the bride. Suddenly that wonderful woman who has become your best friend is "monster-in-law." Pity, but back to my original assertion, when the future mother-in-law is involved, she's usually on first. If not first, a very close second.

So, after deciding who the decision-maker is, the next step is who's paying? If you're lucky, it's the bride's daddy, and he'll just sip on his hundred-year-old scotch and sign the check. Then you factor in that the bride's mother is damn sure going to have her two cents in the pot when hubby is paying. Once the "mom" wars commence, the poor bride becomes a casualty. She has completely lost control of this wedding. The only thing left for her to do is just show up. (This is why people elope.)

Sometimes the gay man in the bride's life can be a godsend. Hopefully, he will be good at planning and throwing a party and convincing everyone else that he is the end-all, be-all. If so, and you luck out with him being the first baseman, it's usually smooth sailing. He isn't going to put up with any petty bickering among the moms or families. He is going to take charge, period. Once again, this is a rare occurrence. So once the hierarchy is established, you can begin to plan this event. And you'd damn well better address the key players and make them happy. Hopefully, the bride can be one of them.

Now, everyone, I don't care who they are, where they come from, education level, religion, or age, everyone believes that this is the very first wedding to be planned in the history of all mankind. No one before now has ever planned such an elaborate event. And we had better understand the importance and what they want because we have never done this before. (In this business, you get really good at that Miss America smile and wave). So let the planning begin.

So many decisions: table configurations, flowers, decorations, music, food and bar setups… the list goes on and on. Originally, I would handle the weddings. Then I learned a very important thing about myself. I don't have time for all that needless bullshit. I stupidly thought that I was the person helping them plan their menu. Little did I realize that I was now privy to every decision that had to be made and dealing with the entire entourage. I knew more about these people than they did, like who was fighting with whom and why cousin Jan couldn't be seated at the same table with Aunt Sue. They chose to use tin cans as flower pot centerpieces because the groom's father has a Campbell's soup fetish. They chose the flowers they did because when he proposed, they were in the middle of a meadow full of the most beautiful purple wildflowers. I'd get the details on how the bride and groom met and pretty much their life story. I'd hear how unhappy they were about the DJ they chose, but he is the bride's brother. Should they have a sign in table, gift table, cake table? Yes, most people do, but good God, they would spend an entire day sometimes just trying to decide that. What should they use for guest memorabilia? Blah, blah, blah, blah… It never stopped! I would spend hours with these people before I could nail down a food menu.

The table configurations were always the worst part. We had a specific set-up which maximized the seating for our banquet room. Every table was an eight top, pretty standard, and it allowed the servers to get around to everyone. We had a party once where they insisted on running three long tables down the room that sat about twenty-six people each. I tried to explain to them that this was not going to work for proper table service. They insisted and against my better judgment, I allowed the customer to be right. The room looked like a goddamn cafeteria. The only reason I let that fly was that they were one of those rare parties that ordered a surf and turf for everyone, so they were all getting the same thing. Sure enough, when the food came out, the guests had to pass the plates down the table themselves. The servers could not even think about squeezing in between those tables. And God help anyone that had to go to the bathroom.

People would drive me crazy, and if that wasn't bad enough, then there were times when I had to deal with the Wedding Planner. The Wedding Planner guaranteed would drive me crazy, never an exception. They came in with their fancy plan typed out in triplicate with every second accounted for, even the timing of the dinner courses for the exactly-timed toasts in between. Make it stop! I finally hired a banquet manager. They could listen to all the bullshit, and I could just handle the food. Smartest thing I ever did.

What Time Is It?

Fridays during wedding season were always a bitch. I usually spent about fourteen hours there, doing luncheons and rehearsal dinners. I had my dog, Madonna, who I usually didn't have to worry about, as there were ample people in the neighborhood to let her out and play with her. We all helped each other out. But Fridays were a whole different animal. It seemed to be when everyone else was busy. I felt guilty and didn't need the additional stress of her wellbeing, so I enrolled her in puppy daycare. I'd drop her off around seven a.m. and pick her up at sometime late in the afternoon. It was an hour break for me, and she loved her puppy play day. One Friday, we had a huge rehearsal dinner, I had already mapped out the plan for the food—very organized, specifying exact times each step needed to be done to have this ready for them at seven thirty. I was feeling pretty good.

I left to get Madonna. On my way back to take her home, I got a call. The boys were telling me that the bride's mother just showed up and informed us that the rehearsal dinner was starting at six. They had double-checked the books, and it clearly said seven thirty. I raced straight back to the restaurant. I mean the pork hadn't even been put in the oven yet. It was five twenty. She proceeded to tell us that she had called Byron and informed him of the time change three weeks ago. Wouldn't it have been awfully nice of him to have informed us? So, we still have seven thirty on the books and had prepped everything accordingly. Now we were going to have to push everything up an hour and a half.

I headed straight back to the restaurant. I left the dog in the car. Luckily, I drive a convertible and with the top down, she was free to roam the car on her leash. Hey, it's bigger than a kennel, and she had plenty of people feeding her bacon. I didn't have time to take her home. I race in the back door and start moving like a tornado. Get the pork in now, start grilling the vegetables. Do everything yesterday, as if there's no tomorrow. The pork isn't even finished cooking when the wedding party starts to show up. Just get something out there for them to start snacking on! At this point, once again, I'm going to kill Byron, and "fucking idiot" was the least of what spilled out of my mouth. His answer was, "Oh yeah, they did call. My bad." Your bad? Are you kidding? This is their wedding! Let's try to get this right and act like you give a shit about something!

Once again, my kitchen crew went into that magic gear, and we managed to have all the food out, and beautifully presented by about six fifteen. One of those times I still can't tell you how we did that.

Ice Sculpture in July

Okay, it's hot in the South. Summer weddings are going to be hot no matter where you have them, and no matter how much air conditioning you have. Doors open and close, there are so many people, it's just hot.

When Val had her wedding reception at the restaurant, her future brother-in-law decided that a dancing bears ice sculpture would be an awesome present. It was delivered that day and set up in the banquet room, center stage. It was some sort of contraption that was actually a shot vehicle. You poured the Fireball at point A, and it ran down the bears to point B into your cup.

That would have been awesome except it was July. July 4th to be exact. That was the day of their very first date. And yes, it was a hot one. I had the staff crank down the AC to about sixty to try to keep the room chilled. Well, our tired-ass AC then decided to freeze up. By the time we got to the restaurant after the ceremony, it was probably eighty degrees in that room. Those poor bears were more drooping than dancing. As the reception commenced, we all watched as those bears just faded away into a puddle on the floor. I felt so bad. God knows how much he paid for those things. I kept apologizing to Val. She had the "shit happens" attitude, as long as we kept mopping up the puddle, so she didn't get her Jimmy Choos wet. Great concept, poor timing.

The Battleship

A really good friend of mine wanted us to cater her wedding on the USS Alabama, the battleship. It has always been one of the biggest tourist attractions in Mobile. A beautiful venue, parties were set up on the bow of the ship. It was huge. She was expecting over five hundred people. She was old-school in the downtown scene, and everyone was going to be there. We knew ninety percent of the guests. This was going to be our biggest catering event yet. It was on a Monday, the restaurant was closed, and our whole entire staff was working the event. The menu was awesome with all the bells and whistles, including a shrimp boil, and a Southern favorite, cochon de lait. We actually rented platters and hot boxes for the amount of food we had to bring. I must say we put out a spread. Luckily, we got there before the typical downpour which happens late afternoons in the spring. Unfortunately, the white chairs, each tied with ribbons, were already set up when the rain started, and the servers were scrambling to dry them and set them back up.

This girl had barely known the groom. They got engaged after only six months of dating, and the wedding was planned just four months later. No one really believed that she was going to go through with it. But hey, it was going to be a hell of a party either way. Our brunch band, Hank and Harold were the musicians. The bar was stocked with every top-shelf liquor imaginable, and there were bowls and bowls of "drunk" fruits, soaked in various rums. The food was spot-on.

Everyone was set up, the band was playing, the bar was open, and the guests were arriving. The groom and groomsmen were there already mingling and drinking. The bridal party was nowhere to be found. About an hour went by and no sign of them. We knew she had rented a limo to bring them there. Where were they? People had pretty much given up on the fact that she was going to show, and it definitely was now a party on the battleship. They had taken to eating already, and the bartenders were slinging drinks as fast as they could. It was like a downtown reunion.

Finally, one of the bridesmaids called me. The limo they rented was too big to get up the ramp. We went to go get them in the truck we were using for catering, which was so full we could only bring them up two at a time. The bride and the maid of honor were the last trip. We had to wait a hot second for that one, as the bride was now in the process of puking in the ice bucket of the limo. Her nerves, and maybe her sense of reason, had finally gotten to her and she was having severe second thoughts. Now we had to scramble around trying to find her a toothbrush. Someone in this group should have a ho-on-the-go kit with them. (You know the one that has all the necessities you need when you decide to shack up for the night, so you're not a complete walk of shame the next morning). Score, I found one. We get it to the bride, and the wedding is now on, we think. There were two bookies there taking bets on everything from whether she would make that walk to how long this farce of a marriage would last. No one liked the groom who apparently had no friends, as ninety-nine percent of the guests were her friends and family. Everyone thought she was crazy, okay... even crazier. We all knew she was cray-cray.

So finally, a good two hours after the scheduled time, she made her grand appearance and walked down that aisle. Lots of people lost money that day.

Banquets

We had one of the nicest banquet rooms. It sat up to eighty people and had its own private bar. Seated banquets were where we would shine. Usually, it was a three-course meal. We had the kitchen timing down. The restaurant seating would be blocked for a twenty-minute period to ensure the food would be plated in a timely manner, then we would immediately go back to regular dinner service. We had done this so many times, we could almost do it in our sleep. But for all the planning, sometimes there is just a wrench.

Since we are downtown, we are walking distance from all the major hotels. Our banquet room was the perfect space for hosting dinners for large groups. I'll never forget this one convention we had for some national teachers' association. Yes, educators.

The group was about sixty people, and they ordered a typical three-course meal. The entrée choices were filet, fish, and chicken. The menu read as follows:

Salad

Signature House Salad

Baby spring mix, red onions, blueberries, strawberries,
gorgonzola, toasted pumpkin seeds
Balsamic poppy seed dressing

Entrée

(choice of)

Grilled Mahi

Basmati rice, roasted house vegetables
Mango, jalapeno beurre blanc

8 oz Filet*

Garlic mashed potatoes, grilled asparagus
Wild mushroom demi-glace

Chicken Marsala

Paneed breast of chicken, wilted spinach alfredo penne
Marsala sauce, grated parmesan

Dessert

Strawberry, vanilla cheesecake

*served between medium rare and medium unless otherwise requested

The only choice was the entrée course. Simple enough right? For banquets, we had that "magic" made up temp that was between mid-rare and medium. It even said it on the bottom of the menu.

So, we get the orders in and go into high gear cooking. There were no special orders on the filets, so we were rolling it out, eighteen minutes start to finish. Awesome cook time! That party was done. Next. We had blocked off our twenty minutes of regular dinner service to roll out this banquet and had moved on to seating tables again.

Suddenly all these steaks were coming back in the kitchen. They needed to be cooked well-done. What? What just happened here? Mayhem in the kitchen. We are already over our allotted time to plate this party and now are overlapping all these re-cooks with regular dinner service orders. Literally, almost every steak.

My servers are so frustrated. They explained to me that when these people ordered the filet entrée, they thought they were getting fish. So as they got their "magic temp steaks," they say (and I quote), "This ain't fish. It's steak. If I'm going to eat steak, I need it cooked. This is raw." They thought filet meant fish. Forget the fact that the grilled mahi was the first choice on the menu.

Shit, I could have gone to McDonald's (which was right behind the restaurant) and ordered forty filet-o-fish sandwiches, hold the bread. That would have only cost me about $40. I'll take that food cost any day. They probably would have been perfectly happy. This is a prime example of drowning in your kitchen. Here we are up-cooking these steaks to "make sure you kill it twice" temp, except for the people who were adamant about getting fish. We had to start from scratch on those. In the meantime, the tickets are still pouring in for regular dinner service. It was one of those nights where you were just trying to tread water. Was the menu really that confusing? These are the people educating our youth!

Surprise!

I was walking through the restaurant one day when I ran into an old friend of mine. I hadn't seen her in years. As we're doing the typical hugging, "you look so good," "what have you been up to," "how's the parents" and such, her friend starts bringing in boxes and toting them into the banquet room. She thanks me for letting her have the room for a makeup event and demonstration that night.

What? First I've heard of this. Apparently, she had run into Byron several weeks earlier and set it all up with him. About fifty people were coming and she had ordered hors d'oeuvres and a wine/champagne package. I pulled her aside and told her that I didn't have any of this on the books. She knew. Why did she talk to him? She should have called to confirm with me. She was cool about it, but a little miffed at Byron. I asked her what her budget was for food was and told her no worries. I've got this. Plan Pull-it-out-of-your-ass strikes again.

I ran into the kitchen and start throwing the cooler doors open, telling the guys the dilemma. We have to put out a spread for fifty people in less than thirty minutes. On the fly is an understatement! Byron! Since we didn't have an event on the books, Kameron was off. I had to call him in to get chafers and shit set up. He just loved that. NOT! Byron! He had a pretty good buzz as he and Toni had been watching football all day. (Okay, she was watching football. He was drinking).

So we start just making shit up with whatever we have. Duane starts pulling pastry sheets out of the freezer and concocts these awesome mini beef wellingtons. That's the main dish. Now for the finger foods. We made ahi pinwheels, crab and artichoke dip, BBQ shrimp and grits, little flatbread pizzas and threw together a smoked veggie and cheese board. I must say the spread was awesome. Much better than the menu she and Byron had discussed. She loved everything and thanked me for throwing this together. You would have never known we didn't have this planned for weeks.

Byron's answer to this was "my bad." I loved how he could say that yet never do anything to help make it right. That always fell on the kitchen, and somehow, we'd get it done.

Get a Little Kinky

Val had a new liquor coming out on the market. It was called Kinky, and it paired perfectly with champagne. Since our champagne was bottomless, there wasn't much upselling in that area. Kinky was available in miniatures, so you could sell it for $3.00 and let the customers add however much they wanted to in their champagne. I loved the idea of it, not to mention the color—it was pink. She decided we had to have a "get a little kinky" kickoff party.

The staff loved it, any reason to dress up. They all wore pink that day.

Lukas even wore a pink bow tie. Toni, in her fashion, streaked her hair pink. We had kinky signage everywhere. Val brought big bottles to use to promote the product. We gave that job to Ava. She flitted around the restaurant with her pink halo, sampling people and getting them Kinky. People loved it. Everyone had their pink champagne on ice. It really upsold our bar sales on Sundays for a while. Then like every fad in the liquor world, it lost its mojo.

Sex and the City

The sequel movie to Sex and the City was coming out. Val planned this elaborate Sex and the City party at the restaurant. All the girls came dressed as their favorite character, and we had a costume contest for best of each girl. She got Moet to sponsor it. They sent a ton of sexy giveaways, wine charms, little pillows, and my favorite sparkly, pink Moet lip gloss. We gave away two movie tickets and a bottle of Moet to each of the winners. She also had a best purse and best shoes contest, which Val would win hands down, so she wasn't in it, she judged it. She was the ultimate fashionista. We had champagne and cosmo specials and played Sex and the City episodes on the TVs with a custom sexy soundtrack playing through the restaurant.

The party was in the bar, but the diners all loved it and got involved in the cheering. The contests were awesome. The judging consisted of how many cheers the entrants got from the crowd. All the girls were totally in character. The Samanthas were even having their own sidebar contest, seeing how many men they could entice into the girls' bathroom. One of the Carrie girls tripped and fell. Did she do that on purpose? Everyone went all out, any excuse for girls to dress New York fabulous in Mobile. The turnout was amazing. Val could throw a party. She was the ultimate promotion girl.

The Food Truck Field Trip

The Food Truck Face-Off was in downtown Mobile filming an episode. They were down to five food trucks left, and one was going to be eliminated.

We were so excited. It was a Saturday, so after brunch, I made the executive decision to close the kitchen from three to five, so we could all go down and try them out. Yeah, I know, I'm such a hardcore boss. I took some money with us to buy food at each truck and make our own elimination. I got everyone clean restaurant t-shirts. I mean this could be our tv debut, especially our crew. I fluffed Ava's wings—we had to have our angel with us—and off we went down the street to the trucks.

Well, we only got food from one truck. It was winding down by the time we got there, and most were out of food, but we took pictures in front of all the trucks anyway. This was a big deal for Mobile. We had some money left over, so we decided to do the logical thing and stop at random bars along the way back to the restaurant and do shots of Fireball. When we ran out of restaurant money, we all took turns buying the shots. Duane had just recently been released on his work release program, and our new toast was "Don't get arrested!" People in the bars seemed to like that cheer, raised their glasses right up there with us. Needless to say, we were a little buzzed when we got back to work. That was fine until about half the dinner shift was over. By then we were coming down, so we kept the shots going. That seemed like the longest night ever. But fun!

Third Time's a Charm

Being as our anniversary was Halloween, it was always a big celebration, some more elaborate than others. Our first milestone was our three-year anniversary. Typically, if a restaurant can make it this long, it's got some staying power. So we went all out for this one. We decided on Alice in Wonderland as the theme. Byron and I made costumes for the entire staff, and we decorated the place to the nines. It started at the front gate where we painted a piece of plywood and cut a long hole in it, the rabbit hole. Once you ducked through the rabbit hole, you had almost entered Wonderland. You were greeted by the hostess, dressed as the Tiger-lily flower. On the hostess stand were tiny martini glasses filled with some tropical-blue-colored shot. Each had a tag with "drink me" on it. Then we had tiny stuffed mushrooms tagged "eat me." The hostess informed you that you must partake to enter Wonderland.

The courtyard was lined with dry ice, giving it a smoky, surreal effect. The servers in the courtyard were dressed as the Cheshire Cat and the Caterpillar. The Cat had a perch on one of the planter boxes and would crawl down to greet your table. The caterpillar was just struggling all night trying to carry food out with his eight arms that were all attached to move in sync. He would greet the tables with "who are you" and "what do you want." Everyone was in character.

Next, you entered the bar which was decked out as the Queen of Heart's castle. The bartender was the Queen, and the servers were heart cards. We had cards all over the wall, and a rose garden half painted red. The bartender kind of got a little carried away with the "off with your head" line, but it was the one time you could bitch at the customers and get away with it.

The dining room was the Mad Hatter's tea party. We made huge papier mâché mushrooms and painted them in these psychedelic colors. They were everywhere. People eating in the dining room were served on antique, mismatched tea party dishes. And no matter what they were drinking, it came in a teacup. The servers were, of course, the Mad Hatter, the March Hare, and the Dormouse. They would pull up a chair and sit at your table to take your orders, offering you "tea" to start.

The banquet room was set as the Caucus Race. We had the big round tables where everyone was seated family-style. The servers, dressed as the Dodo Bird and the Duck, ran around the tables stopping to get random orders from people who may, or may not, even be together. It was funny. The customers loved it.

I even had the kitchen decked out with Tweedledee and Tweedledum, the Walrus, and the Carpenter. They just loved cooking in ridiculous costumes, especially the beanie caps with the fans on them. Okay, not. But everyone participated, and it was one of the most talked about nights in town. Oh yeah, the two main characters, Alice and the White Rabbit. Well, Byron was Alice, God forbid he let the girl be Alice, and I was the White Rabbit. We spent the night flitting around the restaurant, making sure everyone had a fantastic "Wonderland" experience. I kept going through the rabbit hole and checking my clock. Starting a million conversations with the customers then cutting them off with "I'm late" and waltzing off.

It was like dinner and a show. The customers talked about it for years. It was going to be hard to top that one.

The Big 10

The next milestone anniversary, which we went all out for was the ten year. We had made it a decade! That's just huge for a local restaurant. We did this one invitation only and invited our regulars, friends, and family. These were the people and the reason we have been open this long, the people who supported us along the way.

It was a gala event. We themed it Vegas Nights. Everyone in this town, due to Mardi Gras, owns ball gowns and tuxedos, so that was the attire for this red-carpet event. You could wear formal or come as your favorite celebrity. There was a limo parked in front of the entrance gate, and you had to crawl through it to get in. "Marilyn Monroe" was sitting in the limo to greet you and tell you a synopsis of what to expect inside. We had been very vague about the whole night, so this was the briefing. It started with her explaining that once they exited the limo, they were to pose on the red carpet and allow the paparazzi to take pictures. Reporters kept trying to get their story and security was keeping them back. Once through the paparazzi line, security opened the gate and allowed the guests to enter.

Inside, we had all kinds of Vegas-style props and "shows" going on, a very Cirque-du-Soleil feel. The staff was all dressed like showgirls, rotating playing on the props and bringing you cocktails. We had everything from swinging ropes to trampolines. It was magical. We also had gotten a few people to agree to do random shows throughout the night. One of my favorites is when "Lady Gaga" performed "Bad Romance" impromptu.

In the banquet room, we had blacked out the windows and turned it into a casino. We had blackjack tables, poker tables, and even a roulette wheel. And yes it was gambling... for real! We brought someone in to be the "house." Everyone loved it. That room stayed packed. We probably could have been shut down that night, as gambling is highly illegal in Alabama, but our guest list comprised of people that could definitely keep that kind of trouble away.

We had ordered little jars with our logo on them and filled them with our signature blackening seasoning. We put little tags on them saying "The more you rub... The hotter it gets." These were set up on a table by the door so each of our guests could take one home. The food was off the charts. All the bells and whistles. It was a fabulous night! We had transformed our little restaurant into a true celebrity Vegas experience. People still rave about that one. I think we managed to top our three-year anniversary. Like a fine wine, we were only getting better with age.

CH. 6
WHERE'S THE PARTY?

HOSTING EVENTS AT THE RESTAURANT WAS EASY. We were on home base. We had it down to a science. We could do just about anything there in our sleep. Off-premise events are a whole different story. You don't ever really know quite what to expect. You are in uncharted territory. You have to adapt to the venue, whatever and wherever it may be. Planning is key. You have to have a detailed list of everything you need because you only have one chance. Forgetting something usually means you're in for a bumpy night. But even when you think you've got it all together, there are those times when a wrench just finds its way into your plan.

Maritime Museum Opening

One of my favorite catering events was the grand opening of our maritime museum downtown. It was on a Sunday, after brunch. Kameron and I did the "ho bath" then changed into our nice chef coats. Katie and Amber did my makeup and hair to make me look like I stepped straight out of a 1940s pin-up ad. Total transformation. We wore the USS Alabama sailor caps. I must say we looked too cute. The venue was beautiful. A circular-style building with all glass overlooking the bay. We had a primo spot. Perfect backdrop. We couldn't do an elaborate hors d'oeuvres spread due to the kitchen running brunch all day, so we opted for the KISS (keep it simple stupid) theory. We did one of our specialties, roasted red pepper, and smoked gouda bisque, with little toast points. The people loved it, kept coming back for more.

Once we were set up, it was smooth sailing. Getting there, an entirely different story. We never had a great catering plan, nor did we have the right vehicle to transport everything. But we somehow always managed to get it done. So we wrap the containers up tight and hope for the best. Well despite the bumpy roads downtown, we made it to the venue, and didn't spill a drop. They had some underground warehouse area with a freight elevator to get everything to the top floor. We loaded everything on the cart and headed up. Now we were already pushing it on time. We were the last vendor to get there.

Well, we weren't going to get up there very quickly. Apparently, the elevator was done for the day. Clang, screech, thug... it stopped! Seriously? Kameron and I are trapped in this hot-as-hell freight elevator with forty gallons of bisque and a cooler full of champagne. We called for help and waited. At least we had champagne. So we popped a bottle. We passed the time imagining all the scenarios from movies where you rescue yourself. We could just see us busting the roof open, climbing all over the shaft and shimmying up some cable. We were laughing our asses off at how uncoordinated we both are and how we would kill ourselves. Not playing hero, we'll wait. We have plenty of champagne.

It was hot, the air was stagnant, and we were sweating so bad. We had already taken off the chef coats, so I'm literally sitting there in my bra. Of course, this is the one time I am wearing makeup (and a shit-ton of it). I looked at Kameron and asked him, "Is my mascara running?" He laughed so hard that he spit his champagne all over me. Great now my hair too! Wait, who am I? Still laughing he replied, "That's a question I never pictured YOU asking... ever! And yes, by the way, it is." Stupid makeup! It seemed like hours, but really, we hadn't even killed the bottle of champagne yet, so it was probably just about fifteen minutes or so. Help finally arrived, and we were back up and running. Free at last. Kameron headed to the booth, and I headed for the bathroom to try to salvage this pin-up look.

Once we were set up and rolling, the rest of the night went smoothly.

Murder Mystery at the Mardi Gras Museum

I love murder mystery dinners. We have hosted a few at the restaurant.

They were plated course dinners, so I was always stuck in the kitchen, never got to see any of the action. I jumped on the chance to do an off-site catering for one. It was at the Mardi Gras Museum which was a unique venue. You set up the food buffet style on a float. I was so excited we could see the mystery take place. The theme of the mystery, of course, was a murder at the Mardi Gras ball. We all dressed the part wearing beads and masks. We even got to guess who the murderer was, which, as much as I love these mysteries, I never get right. It was so much fun.

After the show, we packed up and were loading our stuff back to the restaurant. It was going to take several loads. Kameron and I were sitting on the curb with the last load, including the liquor. About thirty minutes passed by, no one came back. We realized they had completely forgotten about us. Hello people, forget something? That night I somehow managed to throw my phone away (tracked it to the city dump the next day) and Kameron's phone had died. We couldn't even call anyone. The restaurant was only about six blocks from the museum. We could have walked, but not with six catering boxes.

In the meantime, they were back at the restaurant, pissed off, thinking Kameron and I had just decided to go out or something. No, we were sitting on the curb, still waiting. At this point, we are passing a bottle of Jameson back and forth. Again, laughing our asses off wondering when they would realize they forgot us. We were like two lost puppies. It took almost an hour for them to finally get back. I guess one of us could have walked down and gotten them while the other stayed and watched the stuff. No, that would have been too rational. Besides, we had plenty of liquor.

The Beach Wedding

This was our first big off-site catering event. We were doing the rehearsal dinner which entailed a three-course plated meal on Friday night and the wedding buffet the next day. The event was in Gulf Shores, about an hour from the restaurant, so we booked rooms for the staff and made the weekend of it. The entire wedding took place at a beachside condo. We had to cook the rehearsal dinner for twenty-eight people in a residential kitchen. Now lucky for us, we were used to working in cramped quarters, but this was going to be a challenge. The groom was allergic to shrimp, but the bride insisted that the two choices for dinner were to be filet or shrimp linguine. We really had to make sure these dishes didn't cross. We had brought all the plates and serviceware from the restaurant. We rocked along plating each course without a hitch. The wedding party was very happy. Then came time for cleanup. As if cooking it wasn't challenging enough, we now had to wash and pack all this shit back up. We didn't have time for the dishwasher, it would have taken five loads, so we hand-washed and dried everything. We realized how spoiled we are having a dishwasher (person, not just machine) at the restaurant. Oh my God, we were there until almost two a.m. and had to turn around and set up the wedding buffet the next morning.

Now one would think that we would go back to the hotel and get some sleep. One would be so wrong! We had strategically picked a hotel close to one of the most famous watering holes in this area right on the Alabama and Florida line. We spent the rest of the night partying like rock stars in two states. Okay, it was time to drag our no-sleep asses back to the room and shower off the bar funk to look presentable for the wedding. We might have been dragging, but we were there with bells on. First on the agenda, coffee, and lots of it.

Duane and I started setting up the spread upstairs and cranked up the grill downstairs. Byron and Cody went down to man the grill. We had about 800 skewers we had marinating, in tropical concoctions. Shrimp and chicken—again we had to keep the shrimp away from the chicken so as not to throw the groom into anaphylactic shock.

Well, we didn't have to worry about that so much. The first batch of chicken skewers came off the grill, and Cody brought them upstairs, as we were putting them in the chaffer, he decided to try one. Next thing I knew he was spitting it out in the garbage can. The chicken apparently threw his hungover ass over the edge. He swished a cup of water then puked. That looks great for a catering gig. Yeah, the food's awesome. Don't mind the guy puking it up in the garbage can.

We learned that, apparently, you cannot marinate chicken overnight in pineapple juice. Something happens to the texture, and it became like sour mush. So out with the chicken skewers. We sent Byron to Wal-Mart to buy five boxes of fried chicken tenders. (They actually are pretty good) No problems, only solutions. The wedding went awesome. Everyone loved the food and couldn't believe that we had managed to fry the chicken strips at the house. Yeah, we're that good. Right! The fact was we made it work somehow, fabulous as always. The drive home was the longest drive ever. We dumped the stuff off at the restaurant and finally got some sleep.

The Manor

There was this restaurant a block away from us that used to be the shit back in the day. It was huge, sat probably twice as many people as we did. It had been closed for years and was used as an event space only. The kitchen was as big as our dining room. You could hold eighty plates under their line. Our first time to cater an event there was a little overwhelming. We were so used to our walk-in closet kitchen's cramped quarters.

We got our food loaded in and start to prep. Paco and I were crammed next to each other in about a five-foot space, even though the line was a mile long. Toni came in and pointed out that we could spread out and have some room. I don't think I'd know what to do if I wasn't elbow-to-elbow with Paco. That would be just weird. We stayed in our little comfort zone space. We put out one of the most glamorous spreads we have ever done.

The event was a ritzy wedding reception. The cake was huge, four tiers, decorated with all these edible flowers. It was sitting on a platform hanging from the ceiling with floral wrapped chains. It was like a swing in the middle of the room. Beautiful. And Kameron was going to have to cut and serve that cake. He was so stressed out. The platform was not stable. And the top tiers were a little high. He was shaking, he was so nervous. The guests were circled around, all eyes on him. All he could think about was that cake nose-diving off that platform. As the knife broke through that beautiful icing, the cake started to swing. Then... Bam. The knife hit the bottom, first cut complete. He only had to do that move fifty more times or so, then he could breathe.

The Place Where the Sidewalk Ends

We took this catering job that turned out to be a learning experience, another way to bail out of a jam. No problems, only solutions. We thought it was in West Mobile. We didn't realize it was in the middle of nowhere almost to Mississippi. Literally, the sidewalk ended, only grass, fields, and dirt roads. We finally got there and were led to a barn to set up. Okay, this is going to be rustic, no problem. We unloaded and started to get our spread set up. As we were loading up the chaffers, we realized that we had forgotten one very important thing—the Sterno fuel gel to keep them hot. We were over an hour from the restaurant, and there was no option out here to find a store to buy them. Panic instilled. This food was going to be cold in twenty minutes. The people were cool, but they did not hire us to eat cold food. Good ole Google. We looked up alternatives to Sterno gel. We found one involving tin cans, a cardboard box, and tealight candles for wax. We needed some sort of tin cans. The girl I chose to ask about this thought it was odd but managed to find us some cans of tuna fish. That would work. We hoped.

The directions said to cut the cardboard and stuff it in a roll in the tin can. We then melted the tea lights over their campfire—don't mind us—and poured them in the tins over the cardboard. This seemed to work okay. We did have to keep throwing bits of cardboard on the flame. It was better than nothing. It stayed lit off and on but enough to keep the food warmish. Lucky for us these people were drinkers. They didn't even notice.

St Patrick's Day Cook-Off

One of our regulars asked me to be the chef for their tent at the St Patrick's Day Cook-off. I love to compete and jumped at the chance. There were two categories, Irish stew and corned beef and cabbage, the latter being one of my specialties. I got this. I had spent the last two years corning my own beef for my St Patrick's Day special after being inspired reading one of Julia Child's cookbooks. I put my team together. Me, because I'm the chef. Kameron, because we did all the off-premise events together, so he'd make sure we didn't forget shit. And Sam, because she was the organizer, and she'd keep those plates rolling. Plus, she would get up at five in the morning. I stayed with Kameron that night to ensure he'd be up.

That morning was rough at first. Coffee! Then around the corner to the restaurant to load up. Sam was already there. We were all wearing green tutus and our "keep calm and drink champagne shirts," which were white with green ink. Perfect! We had fake tattoo stickers on our faces, Mardi Gras beads, and white rubber boots, which in Mobile we refer to as Bayou La Batre Reeboks. We were a crew. We got the pot boiling for the corned beef and started setting up our burners. We were the new kids. Most of these teams had been doing this cook-off for years. They welcomed us with open arms, thinking to themselves, "How cute, these girls (and the gay guy) in their tutus. And they are going to cook something." By the way, I was the only female chef in the competition. They clearly didn't take us seriously, especially when I kept backing up from the flame and stretching my arm out to stir with my spoon, so as not catch the tutu on fire. I looked like Tinker Bell with her fairy wand trying to sprinkle fairy dust.

We made the plates for the judges, the gates opened, and the plating began. This was the time where I could finally relax a second, as the food was already cooked. I pranced around sampling some of the competitors' food, sharing my champagne and doing shots with them. Midday there was a parade, and by the end of that we were wearing even more Mardi Gras beads. There was music playing, activities going on all around us, face painting and the champagne was flowing.

The day started to wind down, and it was time for the judges to announce the winners. They started with the Irish stew then on to the corned beef and cabbage. Third place… Second place… First place… Oh my God! We won! I pranced (maybe skipped a little) and got our award plaque. You should have seen the men's faces. They just got beat by a girl prancing around in a tutu. When I agreed to do it again next year, it was game on for these men. They took me a little more seriously.

Shrimp Cook-Off

Being on the Gulf Coast, we are fortunate enough to have fresh shrimp pretty much year-round. We decided to enter our annual Shrimp Cook-off. This was a huge event hosted downtown in the square. We decided to do a tapas version of our shrimp panier (our fancy name for a shrimp basket). This menu item had been featured in our local magazine as one of the best on the Coast. It was tempura battered shrimp, sitting on top of Asian slaw in a rice-paper basket, garnished with sriracha aioli. The development of it was pure accident. We had ordered egg roll wrappers for a banquet but got these rice-paper wrappers instead. After they sat in our storage room for quite some time, we took them out to play with them and see what we could do for a special. Being in the South, we will fry just about anything, so we threw one in the fryer to see what it would do. It turned out crunchy but flimsy. So we tempura battered it, sprinkled black sesame seeds on it and fried it again. This time using a whisk to form a basket shape. It was perfect! Beautiful presentation. Thus was born one of our best signature dishes. It was one of those that once one went out, everybody who saw it ordered one. We knew that this dish would be hard to beat. Game on.

The morning of the cook-off, it's the usual six a.m. set-up (always fun). We got there and started the fryers. Now the health department is always involved in these events, as is the fire department. They were going around inspecting everything, bright and early. The health department made us move our fryers under the tent, so as not to get leaves from the trees in them. You don't argue with the health department, so we moved them. Then the fire department told us the fryers cannot be under the tent and made us move them back out. This is Mobile for you. No one is on the same page. People, make up your minds! We had work to do, and we needed these fryers to be getting hot. Kameron and I were wasting time moving fryers back and forth while Monty and Duane are prepping the slaw and tempura batter. Finally, they decided on the fryers being outside of the tent. Thank you! Time to roll.

We were right on track until we realized that one of our burners wasn't working. I don't know if it was from moving them around so much or what, but it just wasn't staying lit. We needed both since two of our menu items had to be fried. This was going to be rough. There were only thirty minutes until judges' plates had to be ready, which was fine, but once the gates opened, there was no way we could keep up with the volume to serve people. So Monty and Duane go to the restaurant and crank up the fryer to do the rice-paper baskets. Kameron and I get the judges' plates ready and start on the shrimp. Just as the gates opened, Monty got back with the first batch of baskets.

Kameron and I were frying shrimp and slinging out sample cups as fast as we could make them. We were two men down as Duane and Monty spent half the morning at the restaurant. We were working our asses off. We didn't even have time for a cocktail, which is part of the fun of a cook-off in the South. It's kinda like a tailgate party for 4000 of your closest friends, but with prizes and bragging rights. After about ten trips back and forth to the restaurant, the baskets were all done, and they made it back to the tent. With a full crew, we now could breathe and have a drink. I went around and sampled some of our competitors' food. This was going to be tough. There were some pretty creative dishes out there.

Finally, it was time for the judges to announce the winners. We ended up placing second. I'll take it! Second ain't bad, especially since there were about forty teams in the competition. It validated our article as one of the best shrimp dishes on the Coast. We packed up, went back to the restaurant and proudly hung our award, then it was off to the watering hole to celebrate.

CH. 7
HATE A PEOPLE

PEOPLE KILL ME SOMETIMES when they go out to eat. I really do think that working in a restaurant should be a requirement for high school graduation. You'll learn a hell of a lot more real-life skills than what you'd learn in algebra. You'll learn how to interact with people, team-building skills, and to be nice to people who are working their asses off for a mere $2 and something an hour. Unfortunately, that's probably never happening, leaving us to have to deal with the "unresticated." Translation, un-restaurant-educated… no knowledge of restaurant behavior. Yeah, I totally made that one up. In other words, the general public.

Bless Your Heart

When people become extremely difficult, we have a saying that every true Southerner knows… "Bless your heart." Now for those of you unfamiliar with our Southern speech, let me assure you, it's not so sweet. We were raised to be polite. If you can't say something nice, don't say anything at all. "Bless your heart" is our way of breaking that rule while still being charming. It's a way of insulting people without seeming rude. We breathe, put on our Miss America smile and say in the most pleasant tone, "Bless your heart."

Let me give you some restaurant examples to clarify the meanings of this "blessing."

1. You're just so stupid, I pity you… For example, you're trying to explain a particular menu item to a guest. She is just not getting it. She asks for

something that cannot happen.

> Guest: *pointing to an item on the menu* Braised Beef Tips with Garlic Mashed Potatoes and a Shallot Cream Reduction… "I'll have that and a side salad with no onions. I hate onions."

> Server: "Would you like to substitute a different sauce? The shallot cream is an onion-based sauce."

> Guest: "Oh, well just hold the onions in that too."

> Server: "Ma'am, the shallots are infused into the sauce. We can't hold them."

> Guest: "Shallots are fine, just no onions."

> Server: "Bless your heart, I'll make sure the chef takes care of that."

> Translation: *"I'll make sure the chef gives you alfredo sauce. You're so dumb, you won't even know the difference."*

2. Fuck you… A guest has been belligerent and needy all night. As attentive as you have been to cater to their every whim, you are at your last rope, yet you're sporting that Miss America smile. You bring the check, and they leave you less than a 5% tip.

> Guest: *handing you the cash for their bill…* "Here you go and keep the change."

> Server: "Bless your heart."

> Translation: *"Fuck off you cheap-ass motherfucker!"*

3. Just a plain insult… A guest has brought in the tackiest decorations for a party. Among them are painted wine glasses that look like a three-year-old made them.

> Guest: "I wanted to get here a little early to decorate our table."

Server: "Oh, I see you brought your own wine glasses."

Guest: "Yes, I made them myself. Aren't they beautiful?"

Server: "Bless your heart, they sure are something."

Translation: *"Those are the most godawful things I've ever seen."*

4. You just don't like someone... A guest comes in that you haven't seen (thankfully) in a while. She is probably one of the most difficult people you have ever dealt with. You loathe waiting on her. She proceeds to hug on you and tell you how happy she is to see you again.

Guest: "Oh, my God, it's been so long. How is everything?"

Server: "Great, good to see you too." (Not.)

Guest: "Blah... Blah... Blah... Blah."

Server: *Really not paying any attention to their rambling...* "Well, bless your heart."

Translation: *"Why are you here, and I really couldn't care less."*

Beware the Southern blessing... It ain't all that!

Stay the Fuck Home

Let's focus on the customers for a minute. They are the reason we are in this business. We are here to serve them, and without them we wouldn't even be in business. They have choices of where to spend their hard-earned money and we know this. We try to entice them with fabulous menus, thoughtfully put together to create flavor profiles. We have a set style of cuisine and have written a menu that flows with that scheme. When a customer goes to said restaurant, they are there for that style of food. If you want tacos, go to a Mexican restaurant. Fish... a seafood place. Really great ribeye... a steakhouse. Easy right? One would think.

Menus are typically created by a chef who has chosen this as their profession. A chef has this title because of their creative ability to meld flavors. The menu is a work of art. A lot of time and thought has been put into building it. You've got to love the customers that look at the menu, not as specific flavorful dishes, but as a list of ingredients. You know the type. Suddenly they are the chef, inventing their own creation from your ingredients.

> I see you have a paneed chicken breast with a tarragon cream sauce and spinach alfredo linguine. Well, I'll have that, but I want my chicken grilled. I want the mashed potatoes instead of pasta. Oh, and can you just melt some butter with some lemon in it for my chicken… Wait I see you have capers, add some of those too. I would like some sautéed spinach on the side, no butter, just a little salt and pepper and add some sautéed mushrooms. And instead of a house salad, can you slice me some fresh cucumbers with feta and cracked black pepper and bring me a side of balsamic?

> Okay really? Anything else?

Didn't you go out to eat, so you didn't have to cook yourself? Perhaps you'd like to waltz into the kitchen and prepare it yourself, too. Tell the chef all about your menu item, which is clearly better than theirs. Hell, while you're at it, go ahead and fill out this application. It's obvious that you are a way better cook than anyone on my staff.

Oh, the times I wish I could have sent out that application with their plate, just to be a bitch! People, go out to eat and appreciate the menu. Venture and try something new. If you're going to act like that… Just stay the fuck home!

The Zinfandel

Our restaurant was the kind of place a man would often take his girl-friend (not wife). These girls were typically the young and dumb type. You know, klassy (yes, with a "k"). They don't know anything about fine dining. You already know they are going to order a well-done filet and, oh my God, a glass of wine. Who knows if they were even old enough to drink? We would have never insulted these men by carding their "date." Someone has told them about that fine wine we call white zinfandel. To them, this was fancy. It is sweet and easy to drink. Sometimes they'd forget the white part and end up with a nice, dark zinfandel. That was always funny, watching them attempt to drink that heavy of a red wine.

One time, a girl actually got the white part right and ordered it with her—yes shocking—well-done steak. Toni brought it to her, and she looked at it and stated smugly, "Um, I ordered a whiiiiite zinfandel and this is paaank." (Yes pink, pronounced redneck) She acted like Toni was a complete idiot. I mean what do you say to that? White zin is pink! Amazingly Toni didn't completely go off on her. She told the girl she was so sorry and would fix that right away. She came back in the kitchen, dumped out the glass and asked us to fill it with our crap-ass white cooking wine, you know the one that comes in a box and sits on top of the 500 degree oven. She threw in a few cubes of ice, as it was hot as hell, and brought it to her. The girl sipped it... perfect! She proceeded to drink three more glasses... Bless her heart. I hope the date got lucky.

Cut the Corn

I made this beautiful fish entrée special one night. Tortilla dusted grouper with tequila lime beurre blanc, roasted tomato orzo and grilled silver king corn (a specialty that time of year here in the South). This dish was fabulous. I peeled the corn minus a few husks, rubbed it in butter and seasoning and grilled it to perfection, creating the perfect grill marks. The plate looked gorgeous, orzo with that red pop, the fish stacked on the side and the beautifully grilled corn stood up, creating height with the green husks cradling it, a sprig of cilantro and a lime twist to top it off. It was one of those dishes that once you sent one out and people saw it, twenty more would be ordered.

I was having a real pat-myself-on-the-back moment when one of the servers came in and told me her table wanted me to cut the corn off the cob for him. What? Are you three? No this was a grown man in his forties! You'd think he'd have learned to use a knife by this point in his life. Let me get this straight, cut it off for him, scoop it back on the plate, ruining the presentation and send it back out. Do I need to cut his fish in bite-sized pieces too? How about I just follow you back to the table and sit there and feed him. I'm sure I can muster up a bib or something. I mean for real. Who does that in an upscale restaurant?

The Vegan

I have a little knowledge of vegan-style cooking and let me tell you, most restaurants just aren't equipped with the proper ingredients to make a good vegan meal. You need at least coconut milk for some sort of cream and texture and a good assortment of fresh produce, especially mushrooms. There are just so few options on the spur of the moment. If these people would make a reservation and let us know up front that they were coming, it would be a whole different story. We could plan ahead and prepare a great vegan meal, but never fail, they tend to always come in in the middle of our busiest time and test our whip-it-out-of-our-ass skills. So many common restaurant ingredients are just not vegan-friendly. We create decadence with cream sauces, butter, cheeses, and in the South, especially bacon fat. This is why so many restaurants can't stand the thought of a vegan diner. It throws your whole rhythm off.

Once I did have a party who told us in advance that a majority of the guests were vegan. They wanted a creole style menu, with all the meats on the side. So we made jambalaya for the main course. I substituted a vegetable stock for the bacon fat, put in the traditional ingredients and simmered that pot all day. In the end, they seemed to enjoy it, but I thought it was the most godawful thing I'd ever made. Jambalaya needs fat! Some things just have to be made right. Some things just don't translate to vegan. I don't even understand why anyone would choose to eat like this. How do you live without cheese?… Without seafood?… Without bacon? These people cannot call themselves Southerners… Bless their hearts.

The Kids

Now, why would anyone in their right mind take a child who doesn't eat anything but chicken fingers to a fine-dining restaurant? Are you serious? There is a reason we don't have a kids' menu. We are in the middle of dinner service, which offers nothing remotely like a chicken finger. Now you expect us to stop what we're doing, get out some raw chicken, contaminate a coveted spot (in our small-ass kitchen) so we can cut it in strips, make some egg dip and flour mix to coat it in, fry it and clean and sanitize the area we just did this in to return to regular service. Sure, no problem, I have nothing better to do right now. If your kids aren't culinary savvy enough to eat something outside of the box, literally, then just leave them at home. Get a babysitter and enjoy your evening.

On another note, why would you bring a baby into a fine-dining restaurant late night? Do you realize that though you might be used to little Johnny crying insanely, the other people around you came out to enjoy a nice romantic meal? Hell, the couple next to you might have even been planning a proposal until the harsh reality of married with children just set in sitting next to y'all. Not to mention the joy for the server as they get to clean up baby mess. All the goldfish and crackers you tried to feed him, of which eighty percent of it ended up spit out on the floor. There's a reason we don't have high chairs either.

Think about the type of establishment before you come with kids in tow. I mean I know you have the most awesome, perfect, well-mannered children ever... Wait, is that your little angel crawling under that couples' table, chasing the race car he just zoomed across the restaurant?

Gluten-free

Oh my God, if I hear one more thing about gluten-free. I realize and appreciate that some people have a valid concern with this. But out of nowhere suddenly eighty percent of the population has developed this condition. I call complete and utter bullshit on that. It is just as much of a fad diet as the Atkins carb thing back in the early 2000s. People come on. You are ruining it for the people who do actually have a concern about this.

When eight out of ten tickets come in the kitchen with some gluten-free order, we call bullshit on that. It gets to the point where wolf has been cried so much, you don't even believe it.

It got so bad for a while that I reprinted my menus with "GF" (Gluten-free choice) next to approved items just so I didn't have to be asked one more time about it. It didn't really help, but I had to try something. People still asked, as if I could magically pull the flour out of a gumbo roux. And this is where I know half these people are bullshit. After wasting my time on every solitary thing, they still ordered the gluten-ridden items, proclaiming that just a little won't hurt. I guarantee as soon as the next fad diet comes along, suddenly half the population will be magically cured of the gluten.

Allergies

Now I'm just saying, if I were deathly allergic to anything, and I was out to eat, I would damn sure let my server know. I mean just cross-contamination alone could kill you. I know there are rules, and we're all ServSafe certified, but that doesn't mean that the lazy line cook isn't using the same tongs to flip steaks and sauté a shrimp and crab sauce. It happens, and you just don't know what has been going on behind those closed doors.

We once had a woman rushed to the hospital in an ambulance after eating our crab cakes. Let me tell you how good that looks for business. She had gotten through half the second one when she started wheezing and gasping. She was having a severe allergic reaction. I ran out there freaking out that we literally just killed someone. Oh my God. I had not had anything about allergies on her ticket. Her husband asked me if there were red peppers in the crab cakes. Duh, you can clearly see the red diced pieces throughout the cake. That's what it was, red peppers. First of all, as I said, if you're that allergic to something, inform your server. Second, when you get your food, and you see red pieces in it, then maybe, at that point, you should ask your server if those are red peppers. Why would you eat something that even remotely looked like something you are that allergic to without questioning it? And third, many recipes in the kitchen would blend roasted red peppers into a paste to add to other ingredients, so you would never even notice.

Thank God the woman got to the hospital and was all right. My point is, tell your server. When we have had guests that made us aware, I have changed out tongs and serving utensils just to be safe, even though I know that they should be okay. I know I wouldn't take any chances if I knew I was that allergic to anything.

The Food Poisoning

I love this one. One day a mother called the restaurant claiming that her daughter had eaten with us last night and was sick as a dog. Vomiting profusely, she must have gotten food poisoning from something she ate there. Now I do take this seriously, don't get me wrong, but this girl, no. I recalled the evening as she and three of her closest friends went from bar to bar shooting Jager like it was water. They ended up polishing off a bottle of it at the restaurant where they proceeded to order bruschetta for the table, which they barely touched, to try to sop up the mass quantities of alcohol they were consuming. They had a limo, so I wasn't too concerned. We knew they were getting home safe. This particular girl had to be carried to it.

Now we've all gotten white-girl wasted before, but don't go home to your mom and try to cover the fact that you're profusely vomiting due to the massive hangover you have. Don't blame the restaurant that had absolutely nothing to do with it. I listened to the mother and was very polite and told her that I would seriously look into this situation and thank you for calling. I mean, I knew what was wrong with her, and she'd be fine, why throw the poor girl under the bus.

Well, two hours later, the mother called back, inquiring as to whether I'd found the source of the food poisoning. She then started to insinuate that she was going to report us to the board of health. Okay, enough is enough. No more. Yes, I have found the source of why your daughter is so sick. It's black, and it comes in a green bottle, called Jägermeister. Were it not for God-knows-how-much she consumed with her friends last night, she would be perfectly fine. I have the night on video at my restaurant, if you would like to see your little angel being carried out by her friends to the limo. Oh, and the plate of barely touched bruschetta which they probably should have eaten. Oh, she told you she only had two drinks? Try two bottles! Your perfect princess was the biggest lush I've seen in my life last night.

People, that's just bullshit. Do you know how much trouble a restaurant can get into over food poisoning issues? It's something to be taken very seriously. Don't go get wasted and blame the restaurant when you're puking all day, just to not get in trouble with your mommy. Yes... Bless her heart!

The Complainer

You've got to love the people who just want to bitch. Some people you will never make happy no matter what you do. You know the type. If we make a mistake, we will correct it. But don't try to tell me that you just don't like the item you ordered, especially after you've eaten ninety percent of it. Cook temps are always fun. People order a mid-rare steak then send it back to be cooked mid-well with barely any pink in it. Then there is the critic who thinks they know everything. I once had a guy who tried to tell me that we were serving imitation crab in our crab cakes. We literally got into an argument at the table. I assured him that it was fresh jumbo lump meat, I know what product I'm buying (and what I'm paying for it). I'm sorry, but the customer is not always right. And I damn sure was not taking it off the bill.

The rest of his party apologized to me for his behavior, telling me how difficult this man was. He proceeded to go online and write this elaborate review about how horrible our food was and what a bitch I was. This almost cost us a bridal party. They read the review and called with concerns since the crab cakes were one of their menu items. Luckily Kameron salvaged the event. They came in and loved everything, even me, as I made sure to be extra-sugar sweet to these ladies. They were nice enough to write their own lengthy review negating this guy's comments and raving about our food. They ended it with "some people you just can't please." I couldn't have said it better myself.

Mr. Happy

We had this one regular we referred to as Mr. Happy. No matter what you said, he had something negative to say. He didn't seem to be the social type, but he was there every day, like clockwork. No matter what you had on the television, he'd ask to change it. No matter what he ordered, it was always just "okay." The temperature in the bar was either too hot or too cold no matter what it was set on. We'd go out of our way to try to make this man smile. It never happened. We even decorated his barstool with balloons for his birthday one year. He just shrugged.

One day he was sitting at the bar when another one of our regulars sitting next to him started to have some sort of seizure. We called 911, and everyone was frantic trying to help him. We were freaking out! He calmly sat there mulling over his food. The ambulance came and after assessing the situation, took the man to the emergency room as a precaution. After the whole ordeal was over, we were all shaken, but knew he was going to be all right. Mr. Happy just looked up from his food and in the most monotone voice said, "I knew this food would kill someone one day."

Reservations

Mobile is not known as a reservation kind of town. Short of a holiday like Mother's Day, Valentine's Day, Easter, etc., people just don't make them. The one time you almost had to have a reservation to get in was brunch. People finally started making these reservations, but half the time didn't take them too seriously. Reservations keep the tone of the restaurant. They help keep the flow of the kitchen. Sorry if we took them a little more seriously. Sundays especially, we would give people fifteen minutes to show after your reservation time, then we would give away your table. It was never a pleasant scene when they would show up thirty minutes later, only to be put on a wait because their table was gone. Then they would get pissy with us. Really? We are supposed to hold this table until you feel like getting here? It's not like that table may be reserved two hours later for another party. Most restaurants can't make it on one seating for the entire day.

The worst were big parties. People would make these elaborate reservations for twenty people, which takes up five tables, only to have eight people show up, which we could have seated at two tables, freeing up the other three for other guests. We finally instituted seating reservations once your entire party was there. That put the responsibility on the guest. They would start getting on the phone, calling the other people in their party. Half the time they'd find out they either forgot, were too hungover to make it or simply were never on board to begin with.

It all comes back to human nature. Forget the little restaurant that is trying to make a smidgen of profit. Let's be greedy and reserve half these tables, just in case your friends decide to join you, and sit on them all day. In bigger cities, you can't get away with that game. Many will take a credit card deposit when you book your reservation and charge a no-show fee. They are so limited on seating you'd better know how many people and exactly what time. I wish we could get away with that in Mobile. People, reservations are for "reserving" a spot for a time which you chose, for how many people you expect to come, not for half a room, just in case. Take it seriously, or as I've said before, stay the fuck home and invite your friends over.

My Server Day

One day I had to cover a serving shift, and let me tell you how desperate we were for me to have to get out front again. Let's not forget, I wasn't exactly the best server. I was fired from my first job waiting tables. I really am not even that adept at carrying a tray. So I end up in the bar/courtyard area. At least I knew most of these people, and they would understand. How hard could this be?

We started to get slammed. I was running around trying to keep it all straight. I mean put me behind a line, and I can rock it, but taking the orders and listening to all these special requests... Oh my God! I was counting down to when this day would end.

Then I get this needy-ass fourteen top. Oh my God, I kept coming over to the table to check on them, and they never needed anything until I walked away. This table was all the faux pas wrapped up into one. They would snap their fingers at me, and when I'd get to the table, they'd be on their cell phone... rude. The kids were running around acting a fool, spilling their drinks. After three rounds of this, I desperately longed for sippy cups. Their food came out, and they asked for more ketchup... Do y'all need anything else?... No. Okay... I got the ketchup and went back to the table. Then they wanted mustard... Next trip hot sauce... Honey... More jam... More ketchup... Steak sauce... We don't even carry that! They put needy in a whole different category. I must have made twenty one-thing-at-a-time trips back to that table. Clearly, they thought that they were the only table I was waiting on. I was about to crawl out of my skin. The servers were laughing their asses off, knowing I was experiencing what they go through every day.

By the end of the shift, I pulled the two hairs I had left back up and bought the staff a round of drinks, thanking them profusely for all that they do. Thank God for your servers. I don't know how they deal with it, why they deal with it, but they do. That day reassured me how much I "hate a people." I quickly retreated to my comfort zone, my hot box, those four stainless steel walls we call the kitchen.

CH. 8
FOR REAL

THERE WAS THIS HIGH-END CAJUN RESTAURANT out in California that due to the rarity of its specialty cuisine was pretty much booked for two to three months out. It was reservation only and when you called, the menu would be sent to you so you could pre-order your food. I mean this is a restaurant owner's dream. You knew two to three months' worth of menus ahead of time.

If you had to cancel your reservation, the wait list would be called. If you got that call you were told what date has become available, what time and what you would be eating, as you had to agree to the other party's menu also. If this was all copacetic with you—no exceptions—then you would get their spot.

You would know exactly how many people you would serve each night and what they would be eating. Talk about inventory control! And the food cost, absolutely no waste. It had to be so low, especially because the Cajun ingredients were so cheap. The menu was not cheap. They got $12 for a cup of red beans and rice, more if you wanted sausage. No true Southern person would pay those kinds of prices. The whole batch (about twenty servings) probably cost $20 to make. I was amazed by this operation… Wished I had thought of this concept.

Now, this is a rarity in the business. Most of us have to prep the menu across the board and hope that everything gets ordered. We wish we had a magic crystal ball, the one that tells us exactly what people will order and eliminating the guesswork out of prep. Unfortunately, no one has found that crystal ball as yet. It's like the unicorn.

Servers

Servers are key for the prep in the kitchen. They all have their favorite items on the menu and tend to push those to the customers. You can almost look at the server schedule and guarantee that certain items will sell more based on who is working. Now when the kitchen has certain items that need to sell that night (or it will end up in tomorrow's trash) we tell them what to push. Suddenly it is their favorite item on the menu. If we have three ahis that need to sell, it's the best thing ever... Capeesh? I don't care if you hate seafood, sell it.

When you go out to eat and ask the server for suggestions, you aren't always getting the true answer. Now as a customer, you can throw a wrench in this plan by picking two items you are trying to decide between and asking the server which one they prefer. They usually will go with their personal preference or to the bestseller, unless you happen to pick the "favorite" of the night, then it's a no-brainer for them. I've never understood restaurants that have this constant feud between the front and back of the house, us versus them. In my restaurant, we were a team, a family. In the big picture, the servers can really help control the kitchen's food costs. You need them on your side. Utilize that relationship. Your food cost will thank you. It's all about that base.

Cocking

Most servers scoff at the idea of waiting on a table of women. Sorry girls, but in restaurant world, typically, from the server's point of view, we are the worst tippers. This is a preconceived notion that there isn't a man to pick up the check. Now I know I tip well, probably better than any man I'm with, but it's an unfortunate fact, a stereotype for sure.

We had some colorful servers for real. Chan, one of our male servers was a little bit (okay, a lot) of an exhibitionist. He was sexy, and he knew it. He loved to flirt with the women and jumped at the chance to wait on them. I don't know if he coined the phrase or where it actually came from, but he loved to "cock" them. That's when a male server brushes his cock against some part of your body while he is talking to you. He's standing, you're sitting. Where is said cock positioned in relation to your body? Exactly. You get the picture. With just the right thrust and shifting motion… Swish… the cock has brushed you. Trust me, ladies, you're not cocked on accident. It's like a game to them. The other servers are all watching in anticipation, as there are probably all sorts of bets on the line in the back room.

That being said, probably the most blatant cocking incident happened one night with a bachelorette party. They were sitting in the bar area, all these giddy girls, enjoying one of the last nights of the bride-to-be's freedom. There he is at the table, putting on the charm. And yes, the bride got cocked. He won that bet. He went to get them a round of drinks and somewhere between the bar and the back-room bets, he decided to take the cocking to the next level. He returned to the table wearing nothing but his boots, belt, and a waiter napkin, tucked in his belt, strategically folded to cover his business. All you saw was his bare ass from across the bar. "Ladies, here are your cock-tails." He was a ham! All the girls screamed and giggled. They loved it. To them, this was far better than hiring a stripper. He had definitely one-upped the term. I can only imagine the tip they left him.

Ladies, don't say you haven't been warned. Yes, that was his penis that just brushed you and no, it wasn't an accident.

This incident caused us to have to clarify the dress code. We didn't have uniforms, just wear all black. Well, technically he was in compliance. He had on a black belt, black Doc Martens, and a black waiter's napkin. We had to clarify that it entailed a shirt and pants as well.

Fish Fight

Katie came in one day with two fish bowls. She had bought a red and a blue betta fish. She put them on either side of the bar. Now I thought that these were a nice touch, new pets. Little did I know that she had other intentions. They had been there for about a week. I was in the kitchen prepping when I heard a big commotion coming from the bar. I walked out to find these fish in the same bowl fighting each other. The happy hour crowd were cheering them on. I mean grown men! Apparently, she had been taking bets on which one would kill the other. One of the guys was timing the fight. Apparently, there was also an over/under side bet. Fish fighting? Are you kidding? There is nothing right about this… nothing.

I am trying to be the voice of reason, but no one cares. They are enthralled with this fish fight, having the time of their lives. They had even named them. This is utterly insane and so wrong on so many levels. I gave up and went back to the kitchen. Finally, the cheering stopped. The blue fish won. As amused as everyone was with this spectacle, I was not. Thank God Leah wasn't there, or we'd have had another coon situation. The winner took the money and the fish home with him. Okay, guys, you had your little fun. That's not happening again. Amber gets to work that night with new branches for the fishbowls. She had gotten attached to them as her little bar pets. No one had the heart to tell her what had happened to them. We totally lied to her and told her the health department made us get rid of them.

Four

Birthdays are big occasions. I mean somehow, we have managed to make it another year. It was Amber's birthday, and we decided we were going to have a spanking tunnel. She was twenty-six, so here we go. Everyone was spanking her through the tunnel calling their appropriate number. When Byron's turn came, he should have been twenty-two, but he slaps her ass and screams "four" the next person calls five and it started all over. This happened a few times, and Amber never made it to twenty-six. She gave up on the tunnel.

This "four" began a never-ending ass-slapping around the restaurant, that as long as you screamed "four" was totally acceptable. Any time anyone was in just the right position, the four would happen. It was a game, who could get the most fours in. Most people would look at this as some sort of sexual harassment. To us it was part of the job.

#2

Byron and I used to take each other's cars to run errands for the restaurant. Basically, whichever car wasn't blocked in was the one we took. I was in the office one day and he came to get my keys. Two minutes later he came back in the office, threw my keys on the desk, and asked me accusingly, "Why am I not #2?" What are you talking about? He again asked me why he was not #2. Who is #2?

Now you would think he was accusing me of having some sort of affair. It reminded me of the old days when you used to have speed dial on your telephone. God forbid you get bumped and suddenly someone else has your place, your number.

I really had no answer or time for this. I was busy doing payroll and had way more important things on my mind. He meant the settings in my car for the driver's seat and mirror and so forth. I don't know why it's not set, Byron. Just reset it. You are #2. He huffed and stormed out of the office. A few minutes later it dawned on me that I had had my battery changed about a month ago, and I vaguely recalled having to reset #1 to me. I called him to explain this. I felt that I was trying to explain the fact I was not cheating on him. Seriously? I do think he was getting jealous of Kameron.

Strike a Pose

It had been a long night. While the rest of us ventured to our watering hole, Toni and Fynn decided to go out to the gay bars. Now Toni knew all the club owners. She was a downtown girl. Fynn was still the new kid in town. As they were walking down the street, they came across a hot new red Corvette. Fynn decided that he needed to strip down and lay on this car. Keep in mind, he was sober. Hadn't even gotten his drink on yet. So there he was posing on this car in his man panties, and Toni was taking pictures of him. She knew exactly whose car it was—the owner of one of the most popular gay clubs downtown. She sent the pictures to him while Fynn was putting his clothes back on. Almost immediately he sent back a text, "Who is that hot hunk of man laying on my car?" Toni was cracking up. Little did he know that hunk was about to walk in his club with her. Awkward? Not for Fynn. He was comfortable in his sexuality. We were still on the fence about his gayness. I mean, "It's Raining Men" was one of his grooves. Let me tell you, he didn't pay for a drink all night.

Coon

Lukas came into the kitchen one night with a bag of raccoons. His brother had apparently shot them earlier that day. He wanted us to cook them and have a family meal. Now I've eaten a lot of interesting things in my life but never coon. Lukas was explaining in great detail about how you prepare them, how you get just the right part of the tender meat. They have some sort of scent glands under their arms which have to be removed so as not to ruin the meat. You have to soak them in vinegar then boil them forever to get them to start to tenderize. Then you rub them with olive oil and seasonings and bake them. Apparently, you don't eat the old coons, only the young ones. I don't really understand how you could know the difference. What? Do you card them before you shoot them? Do coons carry around a little coon ID? So we cooked them up, and by the end of the night, they were ready. Okay here goes, I tried my first bite of coon... Tasted like chicken.

An Egg

We were getting ready for a huge catering gig. They wanted deviled eggs. They were getting deviled egg salad. Regardless, eggs had to be boiled. Duane asked, "How do you boil an egg?" We laughed this off. Cute, Duane. Here's a guy who can flip eggs to order, any temperature imaginable, even coddled, and no, that doesn't mean getting up and snuggling on the griddle with them. It is a technique of cooking where you slow cook them in a slight water bath, basting them the whole time. The end result is similar to poached, but the yolk shows through a very thin skin. Very tedious. Ask him to coddle, and he's good, but boil? He was serious, no clue. So we taught him a new trick that day. The deviled egg salad turned out fabulous.

Mean Spoons

Over the years I've had to write recipes for the general public for various occasions. I hated writing those recipes. First of all, that meant getting precise measurements. That took way too much effort. Now, when you want some sort of consistency in your menu items, you have to have recipes for your crew. That was not a problem for me. We had our own system of "measurements," a sour cream container, a handful (mine, which translates to about a half for the boys), a dusting, a smidgen, but my favorite was the mean spoon. The mean spoon was our magic measurement, somewhere between a teaspoon and a tablespoon. It was actually a cheap soup spoon, the ones we kept behind the line and used for our tasting spoons. They were separated from the nice spoons used for dining room service... Hence they were the mean spoons. That was always the starting point of the recipes. The new guys had to get on our system.

Push It

We had these beautiful heavy French doors as our entryway. They would constantly get stuck because the humidity would cause them to swell. This made them difficult for people to open. They would struggle with the doors and get confused whether to try to push or pull. So one day we put a sign up "Push." It didn't really help much. Then we elaborated. "Push it... P-Push it real good." We got a lot of laughs and dance moves as people started being able to maneuver the door.

Dishwisher

No, not a typo. One day we were reviewing applications for a dishwasher. Writing, spelling even education are not too important, mind you. Can you show up to work? That's what matters. We came across this particular application... Position applying for "Dishwisher." What? This guy must be good! He can wish the dishes clean. After a great laugh, we decided what the hell. We hired him. From then on, the permanent job description was for a wisher, I mean anyone can wash them. We needed that special touch. I wonder if there is such a position for a kitchen wisher... "I wish the kitchen was clean."

The Flies

Let's face it, if you're in the South, you're going to have flies. They just breed here in the humidity. Especially when you have outdoor seating. There's not too much you can do about the courtyard, but we desperately tried to keep them out of the inside. Oh my God, we tried it all like the sticky strips that only your employee's hair gets trapped in. The flies are a little too smart for that. Then there were the sonic plugins, the sprays, you name it. One day Monty brought in a salt gun and a laser racquet. This turned into a real live video gallery. Everyone was running around zapping the flies with the racquet and shooting them with the salt gun. It was a battle they were never going to win.

Then one day I came across an article online that said if you fill baggies with water and put a penny in it, the flies would stay away. Something to do with the vibration of the penny in the water. What the hell. I filled up baggies with the pennies and taped them over all the doorways. It was kind of a joke with the happy hour crowd, but it did seem to help. (Maybe it was just psychological.) It was the topic of many happy hour discussions for weeks. I think they were even betting on when it would finally fall on someone. Guys, it's a baggie. At least I'm trying to do something.

Then one afternoon one of our most prestigious lawyers came in at his usual time. Now he was the best-dressed man in this town. He had custom-made suits and monogrammed shirts, always dressed to the nines. His shoes probably cost no less than $1000 each! As he opened the door, the baggie decided to take a nosedive. Splat, right on his head. We might as well have hurled a water balloon at him. He was drenched. Everyone about fell off their chair laughing their ass off. They had been saying that this day would come.

I was freaking out that we were about to have to replace his ensemble, which I'm sure wasn't going to be cheap. This would cost me at least the next two days sales. He laughed it off, dried his glasses and ordered a scotch... A double. He was a good sport. Hell, they may have even had a side bet going on as to who the baggie was eventually going to fall on. Needless to say, I bought his drinks that day, and the water baggies went away.

Hair

Let's face it, people, most of us have hair. Hair sheds. It's a simple fact. Now kitchen people have to take precautions. The boys went through a phase where they were all growing their hair out. Duane and Cody had this curly-ass red hair. It wasn't getting longer. It was afro-ing out. They were starting to look like Ronald McDonald. At first, they wore headbands, but we were getting complaints of hair in the food. That was not a good thing, I had to make them start wearing hair nets. That was a sight! But the hairnets seemed to curtail the problem.

One day we were dancing along, pretty steady and Katie came back into the kitchen with a plate. There was an eyelash on the food. When she showed it to me, we immediately knew it was Paco's. He had these long, thick, gorgeous eyelashes that any woman would die for. We remade the plate and sent it out with apologies. The woman was not happy, proclaiming she did not want another plate. She proceeded to bitch to Katie about how disgusting this place was and then went into drama-queen mode of how it had ruined her appetite... Ruined her whole day. For real?... It's an eyelash, lady. What am I supposed to do about that? They don't exactly make little eyelash nets. They shed. It's a fact of life. We're sorry. We remade your plate. What more do you want? And furthermore, how do we know it wasn't your own eyelash?

Well, she wasn't having any of it. She threw down a five-dollar bill on the table (I guess to pay for her drink) and stormed out. I mean I really was perplexed at this outrage over an eyelash. If anyone has a solution to that problem, I would love to know. I still haven't figured it out.

Fuck U

One of our regular ladies, Ginger, got really miffed when I hired Sam to work in the kitchen. Apparently, she thought Sam had stolen her boyfriend and despised her. Every day I heard from her that this was her place and I needed to get rid of Sam. Then I'd hear from Sam in the kitchen about what a bitch she was. Oh my God, they never quit. I learned to just nod and tune them both out.

One day Sam had just closed her gallery and came in for a drink. Happy hour had long since wound down, and only she and Ginger were in the bar. I walked in to check on Katie, saw them, and then went to the back room. Next thing I knew, Katie was standing there next to me. Wait? Is anyone else in the bar? No, just Ginger and Sam. I ran through the restaurant just in time to find the two of them locked up and Sam screaming, "Bitch, I will cut you!" Okay girls. We pulled them apart and sent them to their rooms—Ginger to the courtyard and Sam to the kitchen. This was getting out of hand. Can't we all just get along?

After that, we knew better than to leave them unsupervised. And the feud carried on. Ginger came in one Saturday and ordered a breakfast pizza. I turned around, and Sam was spelling out "FUCK U" in green pepper strips. Then she covered it with a light dusting of cheese. Real mature. Well, at least she didn't spit in it.

One day they met again in the bar. Same scenario, just the two of them. This time we were on it. Do not leave them unsupervised. They finally began talking and next thing you know they were buying each other shots. They somehow buried the hatchet that day. No more messages on the pizza.

Football Betting

The boys (and Toni) were into their sports. During football season they had their own fantasy league. The rest of the year they followed baseball, basketball, soccer, you name it. At one point they set up a basketball hoop outside the back door of the restaurant. They had fun with that until Byron took it down one day. He decided it was too much of a distraction. Now you have your downtime in any kitchen. Would you rather your crew was smoking pot under the vent hood or shooting hoops out back? Just saying.

Duane could spit out just about any stat, odds, or background on any game or sports figure. He was definitely your phone-a-friend on any sports trivia. So we stumbled upon this sports betting website and decided that we would band together and have a family betting team. We called it the 86ers because we were going to wipe out the other teams. Duane naturally was in charge of the picks. I opened an account in both of our names so he could have the check card to place the bets. Every Sunday we would collect $5 from everyone on the crew to go to the pot. I'd deposit the money on Monday and Duane would spread out the bets for us. We split the winnings each week then added to the pot. We were doing pretty well for a while.

We were serious. We had big plans. People were making hundreds of thousands of dollars on this site, and we had our ringer, our sports authority Duane, in charge. First, we were going to buy Byron out of the restaurant and everyone would split his ownership percent. Next, we would each interview and hire our replacement team and take a long family vacation somewhere in the Caribbean. Of course, everyone had picked out their new cars, and we had even found this huge mansion we would buy and all move into.

Big plans! Just as we were getting the swing of it, the website was shut down and our dreams were shattered. Well, it sounded good anyway.

The Flag

Football season was always a fun time. One year we decided to bring in a yellow penalty flag. Kitchen people, listen up—this is so much better than bitching at the servers. It keeps a sense of calm and order to our craziness. Any time they would do something fucked up, we'd throw the yellow flag at them. We used to have a count of who got the most penalties. The servers would make that person do the worst side work at the end of the night. Forgot to ring up that order and now you need it on the fly? Penalty flag. Put the wrong temp on that steak? Penalty flag. Took someone else's salads? Penalty flag. Anything we would normally bitch about, we just threw the flag. Oh, and they knew it.

Sometimes they would try to argue the call, but Paco and I were the referees. We held the power of the flag, and it was the final answer, Bob.

Then one day as we threw the flag, suddenly a red flag came wafting through the line. It went in between Paco and me and landed on the floor at our feet. We both just stared at it like it was some foreign object. Toni screamed, laughing her ass off. Challenge! Seriously? You can't challenge us. Oh, but she did. We didn't know what to do with that, so we gave in. Challenge successful. We had to get rid of that damn red flag.

Prancing Elites

One Christmas, this group of uber-gay black guys became infamous around here. They called themselves the Prancing Elites. They danced through the streets in a Christmas parade and outraged half of the community with their thrusting dance moves and skimpy Santa outfits. Mobile does tend to be a bit conservative. After that spectacle, they were told that they could not march in the Mardi Gras parade that they were scheduled for. It made the local news for days.

Well, you know the saying, it doesn't matter what they're saying, as long as they're talking, good, bad, or ugly. And they were talking. It was enough to get national exposure for the group which quickly led to invitations to perform in several events across the country. Next thing you know they had a contract for their own reality tv show—The Prancing Elites Project.

Season one, their first episode was filmed largely in Mobile. Building their characters was key. One of the scenes for this episode was filmed in the restaurant. They were portraying that they didn't really understand the caliber of menu they were looking at. They said things like we didn't even have a real burger, just whatever this filet burger was. When the server asked how they would like their burger cooked they replied they had never put any thought into a temperature, just so it was cooked. (Okay, well-done) They didn't know what "soup du jour" was and bumbled through the cheese choices. Bless their hearts. Kameron waited on them. Now he was gay, not at all that flaming, and he loved it. The producer got some of our regulars to fill the dining room and be extras. It was quite a production. We had fun with it, and were proud to be a part of their first episode.

Tubing

Toni decided we were due for a family outing. She set up a tubing trip down the Styx River. She chartered a bus to pick us up at the restaurant. It was set. The bus showed up, and it was like a rolling discotheque. This was the party bus for real. We had coolers packed full of food, beer, and shots, which we got into as soon as we boarded the bus. Now we looked like a motley crew, everyone but Marleena. She showed up with her beach heels, big floppy hat, and Prada sunglasses. She looked like she was headed to the Riviera, not the river. Maybe she misunderstood.

We got to the river and tied all the tubes together, with the coolers strategically-placed in the center. We were like a floating island. We made our way down the river to the spot where you can climb up on a cliff and swing down on a rope. They had long since made it clear that it was too dangerous for this and that we could not do it. They had taken the rope down a thousand times, but someone would always put it back up. Of course, that made us want to do it more. I swam around the area where you would drop for a while scoping out the debris and found the spot where we could jump, and it would be clear.

I was going first. I climbed up the rocks and grabbed the rope. As I swung out, I had a flash of sanity. This was insane! Too late. There was no way I would get the momentum to get back to the rocks. So down I go... The spot was perfect, plenty deep enough and clear. Then the boys had to do it. They couldn't let me show them up. I started to think that this might not be such a good idea. They were all working on a pretty good buzz by now. There were no casualties, thank God.

In the meantime, Duane's friend had fallen off his tube. He was floundering around freaking out because he couldn't swim. This guy was 6'2, 240 pounds. He looked like a linebacker. We were laughing our asses off. We finally told him to stand up. The water was only four feet deep.

We found a sandy spot on the riverbank to set up shop. Duane dug a hole in the sand and put the charcoal in and the grill plate on top. Duane and Cody manned the grill cooking hot dogs and hamburgers, dropping half of them in the sand. They threw those to Monty to dunk in the river and throw back. A little sand never killed anyone. We had the spot. The music was blaring, food was cooking, and we were not lacking for any alcohol. Everyone else tubing down the river kept stopping and joining the party. It was like an island bar.

It started to get dusk and we had to make it down the river. Once we got back on the bus, the party just continued. We were dancing in the aisles, swinging from the racks, humping the poles… actually, that was only Cody. The bus driver loved us. We tipped him $100 just for putting up with our crazy asses. This tubing trip became a tradition. We did it several times over the years. It was a fun bonding time, away from work and all the stress that came with it. A family that plays together stays together.

Bama Goes to Boston

The day came when Erica was getting married. We were all so happy for her, even though sadly, that meant she was moving back to Boston. They were planning their wedding in Falmouth up on the Cape. Of course, they were not doing this without their entourage from Alabama. She'd been a Southern girl for years. She even let a y'all slip out every now and then. We booked our tickets, rented this huge house, and it was on. This was the house we dreamed of getting when we made our millions on football betting and moved into the mansion together.

Erica left a few days before us. We were all scheduled to arrive at different times, staying varied amount of days. We did still have a restaurant to run back home. We had the house for ten days. I was there for the duration.

So it was on, Bama was going to Boston. Erica went on ahead of us, but she didn't make it too far. She got to the airport and was stopped going through the detectors. They had found something in her bra. They took her to the back room and strip-searched her. She had decided to shove a little baggie of pot in her bra. The ride from Boston airport to Falmouth was about two hours. I get it, but have the person picking you up bring whatever you need. Since 911, you know they have tightened up on the security. You aren't getting away with smuggling shit. She was detained on some sort of possession charge. Off to jail she went.

Now the wedding was less than a week away. The first round of us left the next day. She was still in Mobile. After a couple of days, the rest of us had made it. We were starting to wonder if this wedding was going to have to take place via Facetime or something. I don't know what her fiancé told his parents. He was Mr. Coast Guard, and straitlaced. It's not like he could say she had to work since we were all up there.

We were getting settled in. This town was like something out of a fairy tale, right on the water with boats in the marinas that were bigger than my house. We hung an Alabama and Saints flag on the front of the house and the "Bama House" was born. Erica's mother had left us these cute baskets with all kinds of Boston and Red Sox memorabilia including games to play on the huge lawn in front of the house. Her brother showed up to bring us "party" supplies. That should have been her plan. I guess she wanted to bring some Alabama shit home with her. Once we got situated, we were off to the liquor store. There were twenty-two of us total. We filled up a cart with every liquor you could imagine. We stocked the bar at the house like we were staying there the entire season.

The BBC (British Beer Company) was across the grass from the house. This is where Erica had worked before she came to Mobile. I got to meet her previous boss, the one who told me I got his girl. I loved him. Erica swore that the two of us were going to hook up while I was there. He was hopefully getting his girl back, if she ever made it out of Mobile. We're hanging out with her family and friends at the BBC, all wondering when Erica was going to get there and hoping it was before the wedding.

Gina was having the time of her life. All the men were enamored with her. I swore they were going to erect a statue of her in the town square after we left. They had never encountered anything like this charming Southern angel. She decided that there was one rule to live by—only talk to men with yachts.

I was enjoying eating the traditional New England dishes. Clam chowder, quahogs, and the lobster rolls. Oh my God, they were amazing. These rolls inspired me to create my signature Lobster Mac & Cheese once I got home. It was immediately a hit.

Finally, Erica arrived, just in time for her bachelorette party that night. This wedding was on! Her mom had chartered a bus to pick all of us up from the Bama House to get there. The venue was right on the water.

It was beautiful. The buffet spread was amazing. She had gone with a mix of New England classics and Southern comforts. She had been in the South long enough to embrace her Southern belle. Y'all and all. After the happy couple was off, we had everyone come back to the Bama House and continued the party.

The next day we decided to get out and explore the area. We took the ferry across to Martha's Vineyard, which was even more of a fairytale town. I had to laugh at the smoking and drinking laws there. There were all these outside bar tables. If you were on the one side, you could drink but not smoke, on the other side you could smoke but not drink, even though you were sitting across from each other. (And I thought Alabama laws were strange.)

It was football season, and the Saints were playing that night. After we got back from the Vineyard, we searched for a place that would have the game on. We found the one place that had the NFL package and off we went. I don't think these people had ever seen so many Saints fans in one place, and probably never wanted to again. Ella was pacing the floor, coaching the team as usual, screaming at the tv... Kill him... Break his kneecaps! And yes, she had brought that godawful mask (Franklin) with her which was posed on the bar. These people had to think we were insane. I'm surprised they didn't throw us out. For real... Who Dat? Thank God they weren't playing the Patriots.

It was finally time for Bama to go home. We had a great adventure and made our mark. Bye Boston... Bye Erica, we'll miss you!

THE END

WE WERE WRAPPING UP SUNDAY BRUNCH, and Kameron and I were already packed for our next trip to Panama, bags in the car. As soon as we could, we were heading to New Orleans to catch our flight the next day, Memorial Day (which by the way is a great day to fly—rates are very low, and the airport is empty). Byron and I had been fighting for months, and there didn't seem to be any end in sight. I figured this break was good timing for us and the tensions could relax. I spent the whole day basically avoiding him, just pumping out brunch and waiting to go. Then he came into my space, the kitchen. We ended up in a screaming match, and I knew it was time to go. I went and grabbed Kameron and said, "We're going, now!" We were off to New Orleans.

We stayed for almost three weeks in Panama in our favorite area, Bocas del Toro, island-hopping and experiencing what each had to offer. We melded into the food and the culture. It was a relaxing trip, almost went off without a hitch. We both had direct deposit payroll and were supposed to get checks during our stay. Well, we didn't. Of course, Byron was doing payroll, and I knew he had done that on purpose just to be a dick. Whatever. We had brought plenty of money and continued our ritual of staying at a great 5-star resort in Panama City before we flew home. This time it was Trump Towers. Oh my God, was it nice! We looked like ragamuffins checking in after two weeks of eco-friendly island life, but they treated us like royalty. We showered, Kameron finally shaved his two-week beard, I finally combed through my almost dreadlocked hair and went down to the pool bar. Almost back to reality. It was an early night. We had to catch the early morning flight back home. We were so sad to go but had to get home. We were coming up on a hugely busy weekend.

We got to the airport and almost immediately got singled out at our gate. Apparently, the flight was way overbooked. The woman was offering us everything and the moon to bump and fly out the next day. We kept saying no, we had to get home. It was Thursday, and we had a rehearsal dinner Friday night, a wedding shower Saturday afternoon, a wedding reception Saturday night and Sunday was Father's Day. If we bumped, we would not have been in New Orleans until late Friday afternoon. Then she throws out the final offer—the airline would give us each a $600 flight credit (enough to cover our next trip), pay for us to stay at the hotel we had stayed the night before and give us $100 each dinner credit. Trump Towers?... That place was over $300 a night! I say yes, let's do it. We'll just call and tell everyone we missed our flight. That's not unbelievable, it's us after all. Kameron was just muttering, no, no, no. The freaking voice of reason. He was right, we had to get back. So we said no, and she moved on. Someone got a great deal. It wasn't us.

We made it home and drove straight to the restaurant. Duane had done the orders and was glad for me to get back to make sure everything was set for our busy weekend. We sat down and came up with a prep and game plan. We were ready, so I headed home. About an hour later I get a text from Byron. "You have been relieved of your fiduciary duties… blah blah blah blah." Are you serious right now? Did you just fire me from my own business? Over text message? You really are taking that extra 1% to heart. At that moment my phone rings. It's Kameron. Byron just text fired him too. I almost had to laugh at the fact he would pull this bullshit move right before this busy weekend, but he did, and thought it was a good plan. Okay, best of luck to you, Byron.

I don't even know which emotion I was feeling, I was going through so many of them. And let's face it, you could have done this a day earlier. We'd still be at Trump Towers wining and dining with two free plane tickets. For that, I was definitely pissed. The staff was mortified. They were in utter disbelief that he would pull such a move in such a weenie-ass way. What was he thinking? Oh yeah, thinking wasn't his strong point. They muscled through the weekend hating every minute of it. They were all threatening to quit. I begged them not to. I mean I still owned it, and that would just be a bad move for me. I had to figure out how to salvage this situation.

Over the next two weeks, the front of the house steadily quit. Byron was getting to be more and more of a dick as he realized that I wasn't going to beg him to let me come back to work. He pulled that power play, and it didn't work out so much for him. Kameron wasn't coming back either. He had already gotten another job as an events manager at our convention center.

Then, one Sunday, in the middle of brunch, with twenty tickets hanging, he went back to the kitchen and dog-cussed the crew. That was it! When he left the kitchen, they turned off all the equipment, in the middle of cooking those orders, and walked out. The whole kitchen! They headed over to Toni's house, she had already quit the week before. A few minutes later he came back in to find an empty kitchen. He tried to call them, but they wouldn't answer. They were done. He had single-handedly broken up the family. But he couldn't break our bond.

Sadly, I knew this was the beginning of the end of the restaurant. Byron tried to hire a new kitchen crew. They just didn't give a shit. The food quality went down. Over the next couple of months, our restaurant reviews went from five stars to one, most of them stating that they had been there several times, but things were different, the food and service were terrible.

At this point, even if I had come back, I couldn't have fixed it. No one was going to work for him and good luck finding another crew like we had. One of the servers even wrote a three-page note detailing why he lost his staff after he fired me, Momma, the glue. We didn't have to worry about the wait anymore, we could barely fill the dining room with people. We finally decided to sell. Too little, too late. We barely got enough to cover our expenses, but at least it was something. Almost two decades, gone!

So the ride was over, and what a ride it was. I knew I had to document the stories, tell the tale of every turn about how we worked together to build one of the best restaurants downtown, including the ups and the downs, the craziness, and oh yeah, the fires. Nothing held us down. I could have told a thousand stories, but I chose some of the best. The family had all moved on to other ventures. Each place was lucky to have them. We have all stayed in touch. We're still the best of friends, still a family.

Kameron and I, we finally decided to make a move. We sold everything we didn't need, packed our bags and moved to Panama. It's the best thing I've ever done. My life is now stress-free, I am pursuing my dream, running a bed and breakfast on an eco-friendly island, with one of my best friends.

I am currently working on my next book… Panama… FOR REAL. It is a true account of all of mine and Kameron's adventures in Panama, leading up to where we are now. It's a how-to, and how-not-to pack up and move to a foreign country. Stay tuned. It's another hell of a ride.

RECIPES

Balsamic Poppy Seed Dressing

This was the dressing on our Signature Salad It was always popular with our banquets. This dressing can be made well in advance and stored for up to a week in the refrigerator. As a meal, it is fabulous topped with anything blackened... chicken, shrimp, filet... use your imagination.

¼ cup Balsamic Vinegar
¼ cup Honey
¼ cup Dark Brown Sugar
1 Medium Shallot
1 Clove Garlic
2 Tbsp Poppy Seeds
1 cup Olive Oil

Put Shallot and Garlic in Food Processor and Mince. Add Balsamic Vinegar, Honey and Brown Sugar. Blend. Slowly add Olive Oil. Stir in Poppy Seeds. Toss Dressing with Spring Mix. Top with Sliced Strawberries, Blueberries, Crumbled Gorgonzola, Red Onion and Toasted Pumpkin Seeds.

Sauce Choron

This is our take on the traditional bearnaise and tomato puree based sauce. It is a light sauce to serve with steak and tosses well with any pasta, especially when topped with some fresh grated parmesan cheese.

Tbsp Olive OIl
1 Large Shallot, minced
2 Cloves Garlic, minced
Two Medium Tomatoes (or Four Romas), diced
3 Tbsp Pesto
½ cup Vodka
2 cups Heavy Cream
Tomato Paste
Salt and Pepper

Saute Shallot and Garlic in Olive Oil. Add Tomatoes and Pesto. Cook until softened. Add Vodka and Flame using a Long Lighter. Let Vodka burn off and Reduce. Add Heavy Cream, Salt and Pepper and just enough Tomato Paste for Color.